P9-AGJ-912

# +

## REDEMPTION AT
# HACKSAW
THE GRIPPING TRUE STORY THAT INSPIRED THE MOVIE
# RIDGE

THE OFFICIAL AUTHORIZED STORY OF DESMOND DOSS

✝

# REDEMPTION AT
# HACKSAW

THE GRIPPING TRUE STORY THAT INSPIRED THE MOVIE

# RIDGE

## BOOTON HERNDON

**Remnant**
Publications

Published by
Remnant Publications, Inc.
649 E. Chicago Rd.
Coldwater, MI 49036

Cover Design by David Berthiaume
Layout and design by Greg Solie • Altamont Graphics

ISBN: 978-1-629131-55-9

# CONTENTS

Desmond's hand cradles the precious Congressional Medal of
Honor bestowed upon him by President Harry S. Truman on October
12, 1945. The medal was lost, along with his two Bronze Stars and
three Purple Hearts, during one of his return trips to Okinawa. The
Department of the Army replaced the Medal of Honor. In an almost
miraculous series of events, the original Medal of Honor was found
and returned to the Desmond Doss Council in August 2016. (Courtesy
Del E. Webb Memorial Library, Loma Linda University, California.)

# ACKNOWLEDGMENTS

I t is rare for a book out of print for 49 years to be republished. This book, originally published as *The Unlikeliest Hero*, is different. As the most authoritative source of information about the life and World War II exploits of Desmond T. Doss, the book was the principle and rich resource for the true story of Doss portrayed in the 2016 motion picture, *Hacksaw Ridge*, directed by Mel Gibson and produced by Bill Mechanic. Knowing that movie buffs and critics would desire access to elements of the story not found in the movie, the Desmond Doss Council, entrusted by Doss to protect, preserve and manage his story and intellectual properties, decided to republish the book after a thorough researching and verification of the factual elements of the book using all available sources. It was decided to expand the narrative with a new foreword, prologue, epilogue and additional pictures.

The process began three years ago with an independent review and critique by Kenneth Lynn, Col., USAF, Ret., Adjunct Professor of Leadership at the Air University. Thanks, Ken—your observations served to keep me objective during the process. Booton Herndon's research and author's notes housed in the special collections section of the James White Library, Andrews University, Berrien Springs, Michigan, were examined in detail along with Herndon's business files at the Archival Section of the University of Virginia, Charlottesville, Virginia. Seth Bates and Michael Olivarez of Loma Linda Universities Del Webb Library Heritage Room were of immense assistance during hours and days of combing through thousands of pages of the Doss Collection of papers and pictures.

Kareis Darling Wagner came out of retirement as a book editor to undertake the massive job of reediting every word, punctuation mark, picture and syntax. She undertook verifying permissions and repositioned the original and dozens of new pictures so that they appear at the appropriate intervals within the narrative. Book editors build bridges between what authors want to say and the thoughts and comprehension of what readers read. Grateful isn't a strong enough emotion, Kareis, to thank you for your contribution.

The entire Doss Council offered support and counsel, but I would be remiss to not mention the steadfastness and thoughtful counsel of Ken Mittleider, the photographic and journalistic skills of Fred Knopper, the wisdom and steady hand of Luke Anderson, Barry Benton's enthusiasm and energy, and the encouragement of Les Rilea and John Swafford.

Gabe Videla, executive producer of *The Conscientious Objector* film documentary proved to be a faithful and valued consultant for his knowledge of the story, and has contributed one of the book's prologues. Thanks to Terry Benedict, director and producer of *The Conscientious Objector*, who contributed a prologue and brought the "back story" to life in the award winning 2004 documentary.

Two new sections have been added. Max Cleland, former U.S. Senator from Georgia and Director of the Veterans Administration, offers penetrating insights into the Doss story with a new foreword. Max, himself a highly decorated wounded veteran of the Vietnam War, and Doss knew each other. Thank you, Max, for setting the tone for the incredible story of this book.

Les Speer was Desmond Doss's pastor for many years in the middle of his life and ministered to the Doss family when Desmond died. His epilogue captures Doss's humanity, humility, passion for young people, and his steadfast faith. No one could have said it better, Les.

Dr. Charles Knapp
Col., USA, Ret.
Chair, Desmond Doss Council

# FOREWORD

## by Max Cleland

W hen I first met my fellow Georgia resident, Desmond T. Doss, the thing that impressed me was his humility, his courtesy and his simplicity. I asked myself, "How could such an unassuming and seemingly shy individual accomplish so much for his fellow soldiers?" He sure doesn't look like Rambo, or the kind of guy you picture getting the Medal of

Georgia U.S. Senator Max Cleland and Desmond Doss shared a mutual respect unique among decorated and severely wounded veterans. Cleland, a Vietnam veteran and triple amputee, also served his country as Director of the Veterans Administration. (Courtesy Del E. Webb Memorial Library, Loma Linda University, California.)

Honor. But when our eyes met, and I looked directly into his gaze, I knew here was a man who possessed a determination forged of steel.

When we talked, I learned that both of us were wounded in war due to an exploding grenade—his during World War II, mine during the Vietnam War. Desmond Doss was a combat medic who refused to carry a gun. He said, "While others are taking life, I will be saving life." One of the stories in this book describes a man whose life Desmond saved. This story caught my attention because the soldier had both his legs blown off. Another medic had left him to die, saying his condition was hopeless. But Desmond Doss said, "As long as there is life, there is hope." Desmond treated his wounds and carried him to safety. That soldier lived without his legs for the rest of his life—but he lived a good long life! I can identify with that story.

World War II was a watershed for America. Without the commitment, loyalty and willing service of the greatest generation, our world would be a very different place. The lives you and I enjoy today might never have been. This book shares an unequaled example of one of the greatest from the greatest generation. If all Americans had the courage, loyalty, and unselfish attitude of this national hero, our country would be exactly what our founding fathers envisioned.

Desmond T. Doss is an outstanding example of what it means to be an unwavering American, and a dedicated Christian, committed to living the Biblical principles upon which this nation was founded. He demonstrated a keen passion for preserving our nation's freedom—to the point of being willing to sacrifice his own life for the good of others. Each time this combat medic ran into direct enemy fire to treat and carry another soldier to safety, he laid his own life on the line. And he did that time and time again. As this book reveals, in a single battle he single-handedly rescued 75 lives!

Those wounded, but saved soldiers returned home, because of one individual's decision and action—Desmond Doss. Those same soldiers had families and children, and grandchildren and great-grandchildren. Where would all those hundreds of Americans be today if Desmond Doss had decided that the bloodied bodies scattered across the battlefields of Guam, Leyte and Okinawa, were not worth risking his life for? Those subsequent generations would never have been born. Those wounded American soldiers would instead have died and been buried on foreign soil. They would never have passed on their life force or fathered many Americans who live in this country today due to the heroic actions of one man who refused to carry a gun.

# FOREWORD

Desmond Doss is not just an average hero, but a hero's hero. That's evidenced by the fact that repeatedly his fellow Medal of Honor recipients viewed him as their hero. The Medal of Honor was established during the Civil War under President Abraham Lincoln in 1862. A hundred years later, there was an anniversary celebration at the White House. Those who held this nation's highest award, and were living in 1962, chose Desmond Doss to represent them for this anniversary. On their behalf he shook the hand of President John F. Kennedy. I'm certain that when Kennedy gazed into the eyes of this decorated veteran, he realized that here was an American who asked not what his country could do for him, but what he could do (and did) for his country.

In addition to his well-deserved Medal of Honor, Desmond Doss received a Bronze Star for valor with one Oak Leaf cluster (signifying two Bronze Stars); a Purple Heart with two Oak Leaf clusters (signifying three Purple Hearts); the Asiatic-Pacific Campaign Medal with three Bronze Stars, and beachhead arrowhead (signifying he served in four combat campaigns including an amphibious landing under combat conditions); the Good Conduct Medal; the American Defense Campaign; and the not-so-common Presidential Unit Citation given to the 1st Battalion, 307th Inf. Regiment, 77th Infantry Division for securing the Maeda Escarpment.

One of the treasures of my life has been that a little bit of Desmond Doss has rubbed off on me. I hope that readers of this book will have a bit of this Medal of Honor recipient rub off on them as well. May we all value and live up to the same ideals, morals, and commitment to freedom as Corporal Desmond T. Doss.

Max Cleland
Former U.S. Senator (GA)
Former Administrator of the Veterans Administration
July 2016

# PROLOGUE

## by Terry L. Benedict and Gabe Videla

M ilitary Heroes are usually looked at as bold and fearless soldiers charging into the field of battle to kill the enemy, performing extraordinary acts of bravery that bring them medals, public admiration and fame.

Terry Benedict and Desmond Doss conversing
at the time of filming of the documentary.

Desmond Doss during shooting of the documentary
film, *The Conscientious Objector*.

Private 1st Class Desmond Doss, an Army Medic in World War II,
didn't exactly fit this vision of the classic Hero. Rather he was a shy kid
from Virginia who couldn't stand guns and refused to kill anyone.

What he experienced however, and what we hope you the reader will
experience, is the powerful story of a humble country boy whose blind
faith, devotion to country and love for his fellow soldiers took him on a
journey of challenges. This was a journey that saw him tested in every way
before being put to the ultimate test of putting his faith and life on the line
in the most impossible of circumstances, the battle for Okinawa.

Desmond's determination to hold fast to his beliefs in the face of overwhelming odds won him the awe and respect of all who fought at his side, then the admiration and recognition of a grateful nation when he was presented with its highest honor, *The Congressional Medal of Honor*.

Learn what truth and faith are all about as you read his story...

**Terry L. Benedict—Producer/Director, *The Conscientious Objector***

---

### Desmond T. Doss
*February 8, 1919–March 23, 2006*

Desmond Doss passed away quietly in his Piedmont, Alabama, home on March 23, 2006. His life left us a legacy of faith that serves as an inspiration to all who knew and loved him.

Desmond's funeral at the Southern Adventist University Church located in Collegedale, Tennessee, was attended by several thousand people and covered by local news affiliates and CNN. Representatives from every branch of American Military were in attendance as were Congressional dignitaries and the Pentagon. His finest tribute came as a troop of

A vintage funeral caisson pulled by two Percheron draft horses bears Desmond's coffin to the Chattanooga National Cemetery Rotunda.

A troop of Desmond's beloved Pathfinders marched into
the Southern Adventist University Church in Collegedale,
Tennessee, to "Onward Christian Soldiers."

his beloved Pathfinder Scouts in full uniform and colors marched into the Church to "Onward Christian Soldiers." Desmond's burial service was conducted at the Chattanooga National Cemetery with the highest honors accorded a Congressional Medal of Honor recipient. A horse drawn carriage carried his coffin and a military honor guard representing all branches of the military stood at attention during the 21 gun salute and flyby by Attack Helicopters in missing man formation. It was a sight to behold set against the backdrop of the outdoor arched burial plaza and beautiful blue sky with patches of storm clouds. The setting was perfect for this gentle American Hero.

Prior to his death it was Desmond's wish to see his life made into a film to inspire young people to hold fast to their moral and spiritual beliefs. His dream became a reality with the making of the Award Winning documentary "The Conscientious Objector." It was our privilege to be a part of this inspiring story that has been seen by hundreds of thousands in special town screenings across America and on National Television aired on PAX,

TBN and most recently The Pentagon Channel. The film garnered 19 film festivals awards from 2004 to 2005 and was submitted for Academy Award Consideration in 2004.

For more information on the documentary, visit www.desmonddoss.org.

**Gabe Videla—Executive Producer,** *The Conscientious Objector*

There was a flyby by Attack Helicopters in missing man formation.

# CHAPTER 1

## THE LONELIEST SOLDIER

Time for the welcome sound of taps drew nearer, and a hubbub of noise and confusion filled the long wooden barracks as the men of Company D prepared to hit the sack. It had been an exhausting, exasperating day. The famous old World War I division, the 77th, had been reactivated to serve in another war, and training was just beginning. The division's insignia, the Statue of Liberty, indicated its headquarters, and the men assigned to it were typical of the melting pot of New York City. Many had been scooped up by the draft in the winter and spring of 1942, just after Pearl Harbor, and were older, tougher, and more cynical than the usual crop of draftees. Now, milling about the plain wooden barracks in various stages of undress—green fatigues, olive drab underwear—they were protesting loudly and obscenely in the harsh accent of the big city against everything and everybody.

In the midst of the racket a slender young man with wavy brown hair sat quietly on his neatly made, brown-blanketed bed. If the day had been a rough one for the older, tougher men, for him it had been a nightmare. He had come into the Army willingly, but as a conscientious objector, a noncombatant. Though eager to serve his country, he had the written assurance of the President of the United States Franklin D. Roosevelt through Executive Order Number 8606 and the Chief of Staff of the Army that he would not have to bear arms. He had naturally assumed that he would be assigned to some phase of medical training. Now here he was in an infantry company. A little on the gawky side, with the flat drawl of the Southern mountains, he neither looked nor sounded like the rest of the men in the barracks.

Not just for solace, but as an integral and meaningful part of his daily life, the young soldier had turned to his Bible. As always he found in it, in the Word of God, a feeling of comfort and peace. He closed the Book and,

Formal U.S. Army portrait of Desmond Doss taken after completion of his basic training at Fort Jackson, South Carolina. (Courtesy Del E. Webb Memorial Library, Loma Linda University, California.)

in a natural motion developed over many years, slipped to his knees at the side of his bunk to say his prayers.

"Hey, look at the preacher!" somebody shouted above the racket. "He's prayin'!"

Howls of derision, hoots, and catcalls sounded through the barracks. The young soldier continued his prayers, motionless on his knees.

The big-city men, irritable and keyed up after a day of strain and tension in a new, demanding environment, were ready to relieve their emotions on any scapegoat, and now they had found one. A heavy Army shoe sailed over a bunk and clunked on the floor beside the pious young rookie.

It was a near miss. Another shoe came flying and another, accompanied by more profane remarks. The man on his knees, though frightened and confused, remained where he was. He didn't want to get hit with a shoe, but he didn't want to cut his prayers short either. This was no time to offend the Lord!

The Doss home in Lynchburg, Virginia, where Desmond was born. (Courtesy Del E. Webb Memorial Library, Loma Linda University, California.)

From outside came the sound of the first notes of taps. The sergeant in charge of the barracks stuck his head into the long room and hollered, "Hey, you guys, settle down in there!"

The lights went out. The barracks quieted down. The young soldier, his prayers finished, crawled beneath the covers. As the clear, mournful notes of taps faded in the spring night, he lay silently in the hard, narrow bunk, his eyes glistening with tears of loneliness and pain.

So ended the first day of Private Desmond T. Doss in the 77th Infantry Division.

The days immediately following proved no better than the first. At night, in the barracks, the ridicule continued. Though he now waited for lights out before kneeling to say his prayers, still an occasional shoe hurtled through the darkness in his direction. What hurt more than anything

Desmond T. Doss as a young man prior to his entry on active duty with the 77th Division. (Courtesy Del E. Webb Memorial Library, Loma Linda University, California.)

else was hearing the third commandment being shattered all around him. The men learned that calling him "holy Jesus" caused him great distress. One tough-voiced, hard-drinking man in his thirties named Karger,[1] who seemed to hate everybody and everything including religion, went out of his way to taunt Doss in his harsh voice. Desmond would cringe. He had never in his life heard anyone take the name of the Lord in vain so brazenly.

Karger apparently enjoyed taking his perpetual foul humor out on Desmond. "When we go into combat, Doss," he would say, "you're not comin' back alive. I'm gonna shoot you myself." Then he'd laugh.

---

[1] All the names in this book are real except for three: Karger, Steinman, and Cosner. Mr. Doss has asked that their real identity be concealed in order to avoid embarrassing them at this late date.

By day the noncombatant had another problem. Though assigned to the infantry, he would not accept a weapon. In vain did the supply sergeant, the platoon sergeant, the lieutenant commanding the platoon, and the captain commanding the company, order him to take a gun. The slender private respectfully refused to do so. He was alternately threatened, shouted at, pleaded with, and coaxed.

He appreciated the position of his superior officers, and he didn't want to cause anybody trouble. It was simply that he had received a prior order from a Higher Authority.

Religion was to Desmond Doss a direct and a personal thing. He had been raised in a Seventh-day Adventist home, had received his entire formal education in a one-room Seventh-day Adventist school, and had been active—fully, intensely, and exclusively—in a Seventh-day Adventist church. His mother, his teachers, and his church leaders had taught him that the Holy Bible is the Word of God, and Desmond had accepted their teachings completely. He did not consider the Ten Commandments as mere guides to conduct, to be followed when possible. To him they were, rather, just what the Holy Bible declares them to be: The will of the Lord God Almighty. Desmond believed that they applied to him, Desmond Thomas Doss, personally and directly.

On the wall of the living room, back in the little frame house in Lynchburg, Virginia, hung a framed scroll depicting the Ten Commandments. Often as a little boy Desmond had pushed a chair over to the wall and climbed up on it in order to study the painting more closely. These periods of religious art study would take place only when his parents weren't home, incidentally; there was a family commandment which expressly forbade children to stand on living-room chairs.

Each commandment was illustrated by a drawing. The one that gripped Desmond most concerned the sixth commandment: *Thou shalt not kill.* It depicted the story of Cain and Abel. In the illustration Abel lay on the ground bleeding, while over him stood the murderous Cain, dagger in hand.

Little Desmond would stare at that picture in horror and fascination. How could a man be so evil as to slay his own brother? Desmond himself belonged to a warm, loving, happy family. His father, William Thomas Doss, was a carpenter who, during Desmond's childhood, provided a comfortable living for his wife and three children. Desmond, born in February 1919, was the middle child. His sister Audrey was four years older; his brother, Harold Edward, two years younger.

The framed picture illustrating the Ten Commandments which hung in Desmond's childhood home and captured the young boy's interest. (Courtesy Del E. Webb Memorial Library, Loma Linda University, California.)

**Inset:** Depiction of the Sixth Commandment as it appears on the illustration of the Ten Commandments. (Courtesy Del E. Webb Memorial Library, Loma Linda University, California.)

One time when Harold came down with a rare type of influenza that brought on a high fever, the rest of the family sat up all night with him. He was delirious and in such agony that at one point his mother fell to her knees beside his bed and prayed. As Desmond remembered it, she repeated the words from the Lord's prayer, "Thy will be done," and then continued: "And if it be Thy will, oh, Lord, to take Harold, please do it now. Please let him be laid to rest and not suffer any longer. But if it is not Thy will to take him, please spare him this pain. We ask it in Jesus' name."

Soon after that prayer the fever broke, and Harold's pain and delirium subsided into a deep sleep. The next morning, the doctor was amazed at his recovery. Mrs. Doss told him how she had prayed. The doctor nodded with understanding. "Son," he told Harold, "the Lord has spared you."

To young Desmond, brothers were to be prayed for. Standing on a chair in the living room, studying the illustration of Cain killing his brother, Desmond knew that he would obey the sixth commandment and *all* commandments as long as he lived.

But though Desmond Doss never looked for trouble, he didn't like to be pushed around either. During grammar-school years, some of the other kids in the neighborhood used to tease him and pick on him. At first he took it. Then one day, on his way home from school, he found his way barred by a whole gang of boys.

The leader stepped forward and gave him a shove. "You're in for it now," the tough kid said.

Desmond felt the cold, heavy ball of fear in the pit of his stomach. He knew he was in for a beating, but he resolved to get as many as he could before he went down. Suddenly he charged, swinging his fists wildly. The attack took the leader of the gang completely by surprise. He broke and ran. That was the end of the fight, and from then on Desmond's peers treated him with respect.

Baseball was the most popular sport in Lynchburg during Desmond's childhood. The kids began tossing balls back and forth on the first sunny day of early spring, and continued playing all summer long. Desmond enjoyed playing as much as anyone else until the day, when he was eight years old, he fell and cut his hand on a broken bottle. The jagged glass sliced through several tendons, all across the palm of his hand.

The family doctor looked at it, tested the dangling fingers, and shook his head sadly. "You'll never be able to use this hand again, Desmond," he said.

Desmond's mother did not give up so easily. When the cut was healed, she began massaging his injured hand, moving his fingers. With her help and encouragement he regained the use of his fingers. But the scar, which ran completely across the palm, remained sensitive. He could no longer participate in any sport requiring two good hands.

At first young Desmond was crushed. But as the days went on, he found there were other things a high-spirited youngster could do besides play games. Rather than sit and mope around the house, he did more than his share of the household chores. His mother loved flowers, and he would work with her by the hour, helping her and nature create beauty. They had so many flowers that they began sharing them with others less fortunate. At first they gave flowers to their neighbors, especially when someone happened to be sick. People were so appreciative that Desmond also began taking flowers to the hospital and even to the city jail. Sharing beauty, he discovered, was even better than raising it.

The visits were not always pleasant. One patient—an indigent, aged man with no friends or relatives left in the world—was dying with an incurable disease. He could not afford a nurse, and Desmond volunteered to stay with him. The pain the poor old man suffered was so intense that Desmond could almost feel the hurt himself. He couldn't stand it and ran out to get the doctor.

"Please give him something for the pain!" the boy pleaded.

The doctor patted him on the shoulder. "I've already given him a massive dose," he said. "I can't give him any more."

That night death spared the patient further misery. Desmond went home, but he could not sleep. He could still hear those cries and groans of pain. However, the boy did not regret having been at the old man's bedside. He had done what he could; the patient had not died alone and friendless.

The boy had learned that even in such an unhappy situation there can be a positive feeling of satisfaction from having done the best he could to help a fellow human being. This was in itself a reward.

But sometimes more positive good resulted. One Sabbath, church services were interrupted for an announcement that a woman, a former member, was in desperate need of a blood transfusion. Desmond, along with several members of the congregation, hurried to the hospital. No one mentioned the fact that neither the woman nor her husband attended the church. They were Adventists, but there had been some misunderstanding when they moved to Lynchburg some time before. They thought they were not welcome at the church, and then it became a matter of pride to stay away.

It was Desmond's blood, and his only, which matched that of the ill woman. He was only a skinny boy in his early teens, but the patient's condition was critical, and he offered his blood without hesitation. After giving it, he got off the table on which he had been lying and had to grab a hatrack to keep from falling to the floor.

The woman pulled through. She and her husband asked Desmond to come see them. They offered first to pay him, then, when he refused, asked if they could not give him some kind of present.

"Yes, you can give me a present," the boy said. "Come to church."

They did, and became active, dedicated members of the congregation.

With this background, Desmond Doss was poured into the mold of the model medical soldier of the United States Army. The higher echelons of the military establishment in Washington were fully aware of the existence of men like Doss and had established an official policy to use them. A quarter of a century before, in World War I, bona fide conscientious objectors had been mistreated and imprisoned. Men were kicked, beaten, and dunked headfirst into latrines. During the war, 162 members of the Seventh-day Adventist Church alone were court-martialed because of their religious convictions, and when the war ended thirty-five of these men were serving terms of from five to twenty years at hard labor. Thanks to tireless efforts on the part of religious leaders, and to the American tradition of religious freedom, all of these men were given full pardons on Armistice Day, 1918.

In the period between wars interest increased in the question of how the young Adventist could serve his country, as he is specifically adjured to do in Romans 13:1, and yet obey the sixth commandment. An elaborate program developed in which the church and the armed services cooperated to enable Adventists to serve where they were best suited, in the medical department. In 1934 the Adventists organized a Medical Cadet Corps to train their youth of preservice age in the fundamentals of military medical service. Several Adventist colleges and academies in the United States and other countries set up MCC units. The accent was on service to the nation within the framework of religious belief. In recognition of the valuable service which can be rendered by young men eager to serve their country, but without taking human life, the Congress of the United States specifically wrote into the military draft law the provision that conscientious objectors be assigned to the medical department.

Desmond Doss was fully aware of the situation. He registered for the draft along with the other young men of Lynchburg, and was classified I-A-O. The "O" stood for "conscientious objector," and Desmond put in a mild protest to his draft board about it.

"I'm not a conscientious objector," he said. "I'm willing to serve. What I am is a noncombatant."

"There isn't any such classification," he was told. "You're in I-A-O and that's where you're going to stay."

According to the official procedure worked out by the church and the armed services, Adventists would not volunteer for service, but would wait their turn in the draft. While waiting, Desmond had worked in a shipyard, a vital war industry, and had taken a course in first aid to prepare himself for service when the call came. When it did come, a shipyard official suggested to him that he could seek deferment on the grounds of being essential to industry. He refused even to consider it.

"I'm not essential here, and you know it," he said.

Many of Desmond's friends enlisted. Several were classified 4-F, unfit for military service. There were those who took their own lives out of disappointment and embarrassment over not being able to serve their country. Desmond was profoundly affected. Despite his mother's pleadings, and his father's objections, Desmond, desperately wanting to do his patriotic duty, enlisted in the Army and entered military service April 1, 1942, at Camp Lee, Virginia. Instead of being sent to basic training in the medical department, however, he found himself with the newly reactivated 77th Division at Fort Jackson, South Carolina. The men were to train as a unit. In the confusion of those early days, Desmond Doss, draft classification I-A-O, was stuck in a rifle company.

There is a saying in the Army, whenever anybody complains—"Go tell it to the chaplain." That is exactly what Doss did. The chaplain, Captain Carl Stanley, received him warmly and listened to his story. Captain Stanley had a close friend in the ministry of the Seventh-day Adventist Church, and he was well acquainted with the customs and beliefs of this comparatively small, but extremely active, Protestant denomination. He knew that this soldier was a bona fide objector and as such entitled by law to be assigned to the medical department. Captain Stanley explained the situation at division headquarters. Desmond was placed in the medics where he belonged and began his training as a medical soldier.

Military medicine is a kind of advanced first aid, applicable to the battlefield. Desmond learned the contents of his two large canvas first-aid kits, and the specific use of each item. There were the battle dressings of various sizes to be placed over open wounds. There were packages of sulfanilamide powder to be sprinkled over open wounds before the dressing was put in place. There were syrettes of morphine to be injected to alleviate the pain. Desmond learned not only how to make the injection, but, of equal importance, when to use the drug and when not. In some types of wounds morphine can be fatal.

With the other rookie medics, he learned how to use whatever material was at hand—saplings, rifle stocks—to make splints for broken limbs. He learned how to give blood plasma on the battlefield, what to do for shock, when to administer water and when to withhold it. It was like going to school again. Desmond remembered the little brown-shingled school operated by the church back in Lynchburg. There was only one teacher for eight grades, but each grade contained only a few children. The teacher would work with each class in turn. Desmond recalled how, when it was time for his group to recite, they would move up to the desks in the first row. That brought them closer not only to the teacher, but also to the warm, potbellied stove in the front of the room. On chilly days in winter, every child looked forward to the recitation period.

Who does not remember his first schoolteacher? Desmond could never forget Mrs. Nell Ketterman, who, after his mother, was the greatest inspiration of his life. When the boy had been too shy to recite in class, it was Mrs. Ketterman who encouraged him. When he had despaired of making legible figures, it was Mrs. Ketterman who stayed after school with him, urging him with warmth and love and understanding to guide his pencil over the paper again and again and again until what had resembled chicken scratches became numerals and letters, clear and unmistakable.

One day it was Desmond's turn to wash the blackboards and dust the chalk off the erasers. He had perfunctorily hit the erasers together a few times and put them down. That did not satisfy Mrs. Ketterman.

"If a job is worth doing, it's worth doing right," she told him. It was the first time he had heard that simple philosophy, but not the last. It became so embedded in his brain that forever after he could play it back like a phonograph record. *If a job is worth doing, it's worth doing right.* Those words became a part of his life.

Desmond had been unable to continue school after the eighth grade. The Depression that came in with the thirties made it difficult for his father to obtain work, and Desmond had to pitch in to help support the family. He found a job in a lumberyard doing rough, heavy work for ten cents an hour, fifty hours a week. Of that five dollars he gave fifty cents to the church as his tithe and $3 to his mother. He spent 50 cents a week for carfare and with the remaining dollar bought all of his clothing and necessities.

Though regular school was over for him, he continued to go to Sabbath School. On the wall of the Sabbath School room hung a large picture of the Sea of Galilee. Each pupil could place on it little boat-like stickers for being present and on time, knowing the lesson, and knowing the memory verse. For an additional incentive, if you could say all of the memory verses for an entire three months, you would get a Bible. For each quarter of perfect attendance the award was a bookmark. When he was just a youngster, Desmond missed one session, and that wiped out his attendance record for the entire quarter. From then on he never missed, nor did he ever fail to prepare his lesson.

One day the family visited relatives out of town and didn't get back until late at night. The next day was the Sabbath, and Desmond had not prepared his lesson. Though he was so tired and sleepy he could barely make out the words, he still stayed up and completed the assignment. In the morning he dragged his weary body out of bed and to Sabbath School. He had worked too many hours preparing his lessons over the preceding part of the year, had unfailingly attended too many Sabbath School sessions, to permit one lapse to cost him the benefits and rewards of perfect attendance. He was protecting his investment of time and study.

In this way, to Desmond Doss, conscientious attention to duty became a way of life. Sometimes, at Fort Jackson, in an afternoon class on a hot day following a morning of vigorous exercise and a heavy midday dinner, with an instructor droning away on how to purify water or how flies can carry disease, some of the men would start to nod. Not Desmond. He was there, he stayed awake, and he listened. It was his way of life.

Would you not believe, then, that this earnest, attentive medical soldier would have earned the respect and admiration of his officers, if not his fellow recruits? Instead, he was considered an oddball, a headache, a troublemaker by his officers, even up to the headquarters of the regiment.

Why were they down on him when he tried to be an exemplary soldier, a "conscientious cooperator" rather than an objector, in everything his religion did not forbid?

There were several strikes against him. Prejudice against conscientious objectors prevailed, and although Desmond hated to admit it, he could see why. There were three other "conchies" in the division, and Desmond had no use for any of them. He was eager to serve his country in a noncombatant capacity, but these three guys wanted no part of military life, period. Their only dedication was to the avoidance of work. And one of them, whose teeth were black from snuff, was downright repulsive. One day they were no longer with the division, for which everyone was thankful, but in the meantime, Desmond suffered through association.

"You guys are all alike," one of his sergeants accused him. "You talk big about religious freedom, but when your country needs you to help protect that freedom you chicken out."

"That's where you're wrong, sergeant," Desmond said earnestly. "In my church we're taught to obey government authority, just like the Bible says. You'll never find me failing to salute the flag or trying to get out of a detail. I love this country just as much as you do."

Sometimes when the infantry marched out to the rifle range to spend the day in marksmanship training, Desmond would go along. But of course he would not participate. The hot, hard-working riflemen down on the shooting line, blasting off round after round until their ears rang and their shoulders ached, saw their medic standing around doing nothing, and naturally they resented him.

But the main reason for Desmond's unpopularity was his insistence on keeping the fourth commandment.

"Remember the Sabbath day, to keep it holy," the Lord told Moses some 3,500 years ago, and Desmond, as we have seen, heeded the Word of God as he understood it. Those words applied to the human race in general and to him, Desmond Doss, in particular. No one—neither the commander of the battalion, the regiment, or the division, nor the President of the United States—could make Desmond Doss disobey a commandment given him by God. The only exception to the fourth commandment was that put forward by the Son of God, Jesus Christ. Desmond's Bible had told him that Christ had healed the sick on the Sabbath. Desmond was also more than willing on the Sabbath to help sick people and, in combat, the wounded.

But there in South Carolina, thousands of miles from the fighting front, the sick were taken to the hospital and there were no wounded. Desmond could see no conceivable reason for disobeying the fourth commandment.

What made life especially difficult there in the 77th Division was the fact that Desmond, as a Seventh-day Adventist, did not observe Sunday, the first day of the week, but Saturday, the seventh. *Six days shalt thou labor, and do all thy work: but the seventh day is the Sabbath of the Lord thy God: in it thou shalt not do any work.* Desmond had known these words by heart almost as long as he could remember.

The 77th Division, of course, and the rest of the Armed Forces, recognized Sunday both as a day of rest and a day of worship. Practically all activities at Fort Jackson terminated Saturday afternoon and were not resumed until Monday morning. There was a chapel on the post with services for both Catholics and Protestants. Every large unit had its own chaplain who could hold services right there. Maneuvers were usually scheduled to terminate before Sunday, but if they did continue through the weekend, provision was made to hold Sunday services in the field.

As a seventh-day observer in a first-day Army, therefore, Desmond found himself doubly out of step. First, his religion forbade him to work from sundown Friday until sundown Saturday, which necessitated being officially excused from every operation during that period, every week. And second, because there were no Christian services held on the post on Saturday, he had to secure a pass to go into town to attend services there. These services usually included a young people's meeting Friday night and regular church services Saturday morning.

It quickly became evident that in the matter of the United States Army versus Private Desmond T. Doss over the issue of the Sabbath, one of the two must back down, and it would not be Desmond. His first altercation over this matter occurred on his second day in the Army. He was inducted on a Friday. Saturday morning the sergeant ordered everybody to start scrubbing the barracks floor for Saturday inspection. Desmond refused to participate. He had come into the Army prepared to perform necessary duties on the Sabbath, as he believed Christ had done. But scrubbing the floor was not, in his mind, a necessary duty. A floor can be scrubbed any day in the week. It was certainly not going to be scrubbed the next day, Sunday.

The sergeant called in the lieutenant. The lieutenant couldn't get anywhere with the stubborn Sabbath keeper either, and angrily told him to get out of the barracks. Doss stepped outside, but a major came along and ordered him back in. He spent his first Sabbath in the Army huddled in a corner of the barracks while the other men, working, invented nasty remarks and passed them along to him gratis.

It was the same thing all over again when he joined the 77th Division. On his first Friday he consulted the chaplain about getting a pass to go into Columbia to church. The chaplain, Captain Stanley, pointed out that regulations prohibited giving any man a pass for any reason during his first two weeks in the camp.

"I believe that God will work out a way for me to go to church," Private Doss told the chaplain.

Captain Stanley sighed. He knew those Seventh-day Adventists. "I'll see what I can do at division headquarters," he said. That afternoon the pass came through.

By the next week Desmond had been transferred from the rifle company to the medical battalion. He reported to the battalion CO, Major Fred Steinman,[2] to ask for a pass to go to church on Saturday. The major's concern was with the training of a battalion. He gave Desmond his pass, but when he continued to come back week after week, the officer became annoyed. "This is the last one," he warned one Friday. "Don't come back for any more."

Desmond knew the major meant it. He asked the people in church next day to pray for him. And on the following Friday he asked for another pass. The major blew up and told him to get out. Again Desmond went to Captain Stanley. The chaplain took the matter up with division headquarters and it was determined that the Adventist soldier would have his Saturdays off just as the other men had their Sundays. Desmond had won except that in the Army it is not wise for privates to win over majors.

In actuality Desmond was never any better off than anybody else. In exchange for his Saturdays off, he pulled special duty on Sunday, all day Sunday. But none of the other men were around to see him that day and resented his Saturday freedom just the same. "You get more passes than the general," they complained.

The reaction among the infantrymen was especially bitter. There were the differences in speech and habits, his idleness at the rifle range, and now this special privilege. News of the strange soldier spread throughout the regiment. One day Desmond ran into Karger, that hard, cynical older man in Company D who had taken such delight in tormenting him before.

"You think you're so holy, Doss," Karger told him, adding some expletives. "Well, when we get in combat I'm gonna shoot you down like a dog."

It's not easy to live with men who hate you, especially when your sole mission is learning to care for those very men. This was a lonely, frustrating period for Private Doss.

At such a time a man turns not to his mother, not to his minister, not to the chaplain. He tells his troubles to his girl.

Desmond's girl was pretty, blond, serious, and, like him, a devout Seventh-day Adventist. Her name was Dorothy Schutte, and she was from Richmond, Virginia. She was one of seven children of a disabled veteran of World War I, and the family barely got by on his pension. Dorothy had

---

2   A pseudonym.

determined to make something of her life. The first thing she must do, she realized, was get an education. That required money. When she was still in high school she got a job as a colporteur, selling Adventist books. Desmond met her when she came through Lynchburg. He and his family extended a normal amount of southern—plus Adventist—hospitality; they took her for a drive one Sabbath afternoon.

That fall Dorothy attended Washington Missionary College in Washington, D.C. She supported herself by working as a domestic in the home of a Washington family. Her work kept her from carrying a full scholastic schedule, but she didn't complain. She was on her way.

Adventists form a close group, something like a large family, and it was perfectly natural for Desmond to keep hearing of this ambitious young woman who was determined to get an education. She was the kind of girl he would like to know better.

Desmond had never had a sweetheart. He had gone around with groups of young Adventists, but had never become interested in one girl. He had made up his mind to save his love and his affection for the girl he would marry. He was twenty-two years old before he gathered up his courage and sought his first date. Before his induction he was working in a shipyard in Newport News, Virginia, for one dollar an hour; he had a secondhand car; he was rich. One Saturday morning he drove the 200 miles to Washington hoping to see Dorothy Schutte.

People were just beginning to enter Columbia Hall, the college chapel, for Sabbath services when he arrived. He looked for her but didn't see her. Finally services began, and he went on into the chapel and took a seat. There, right in front of him, sat Dorothy! He leaned forward and whispered Hello, but she shushed him without turning around. He had driven 200 miles for a "Sh-h-h!"

After the services, the congregation gathered in groups outside to talk. Dorothy was standing with a young married couple she knew. Desmond joined her just as they were inviting her to dinner.

"She's having dinner with me!" Desmond blurted.

Dorothy shot him a quick look, but she did not correct him. They did have dinner together, and all that afternoon, and supper too.

Desmond was well known as one of the young lay leaders of the church. He and Dorothy had several interests in common, and a great many mutual friends, and the conversation never flagged. He had intended to go on back to Newport News that day, but he put that thought out of his mind. He had found her now. He stayed over and spent Sunday with her, too, until it was time for her to prepare her lessons. For once Desmond disapproved of conscientiousness. But Dorothy said she would be happy to see him again, and Desmond sang all the way back to Newport News.

From then on, Desmond drove to Washington every other weekend. Several visits later, he and Dorothy double-dated with another Adventist couple. Desmond and Dorothy were in the back seat, and, driving through Rock Creek Park, he kissed her. He was lucky she didn't knock his head off, because she was furious. Her face turned a flaming red. She had never been kissed before. Like Desmond, she was saving her love and affection for the person she would marry.

Desmond saw the look on her face. "I love you," he said quickly. It was the first time he had said those words. That made the kiss all right. For, Dorothy confessed, she loved him too.

But he was in no position to propose. They had discussed wartime marriages, and both opposed them. Desmond knew he would be called into service any day. When the notice came from the draft board, he made the last visit to Washington to see her.

"Will you wait for me?" he asked.

"Yes, I will," she said. Those were the most wonderful words he had ever heard.

They spent the rest of Desmond's last date with her as a civilian talking about the life they would lead after the war. It was amazing how similar their dreams were. Neither wanted a big house, or riches. They would both be satisfied with the most humble home as long as it was a Christian home. They resolved to have family worship every morning and every night. They both wanted lots of children to love and to bring up in the Christian faith.

They parted tearfully but bravely. Both felt sure they were doing the right thing.

As the lonely weeks at Fort Jackson went by, as Desmond found his misery increasing, the letters from Dorothy became more and more important. They encouraged him to keep going. Her love for him was the sole comfort in his friendless existence. He asked her to come to Columbia on a weekend, and she did, staying with an Adventist family he had met at church. They spent a warm and happy Sabbath together. This time the leave-taking was not so easy.

On the long Fourth of July weekend Desmond took the long bus ride to Richmond to surprise her. When he arrived, he learned that she had gone to Columbia to surprise him. They could continue to cross paths for days, so Desmond stayed put. Dorothy meanwhile had learned that he had gone to Richmond, and caught the next train back. They still had two days together.

Gradually Dorothy and Desmond realized that they did not want to wait until after the war was over. Both discussed their problems with their ministers, and they were advised to do what they thought best. That was the answer they wanted, for what they thought best was to be together, as man and wife, every possible minute. Dorothy and her mother began arranging for a wedding at their church.

Desmond and Dorothy Doss on their wedding day
in Richmond, Virginia, 1942. (Courtesy Del E. Webb
Memorial Library, Loma Linda University, California.)

But Desmond's commanding officers had no intention of letting this Seventh-day troublemaker go off and get married. No one would give him a definite answer to his request for a furlough. In desperation Desmond went over the head of the battalion commander, to the regimental adjutant. He was waiting there when in came the commander of the regiment, Colonel William H. Craig, the silver eagles of his rank gleaming. He was the highest-ranking officer Desmond had ever seen, and the most formidable.

"Is there anything I can do for you, soldier?" the colonel asked.

"If anybody can, you can," Desmond said, quickly adding, "Sir! I want to get married!"

The colonel listened to Desmond's story and apparently decided that he was sincere. He picked up the telephone and called the medical battalion.

"Why can't this man get married?" the colonel demanded. "When a man makes up his mind to get married you might as well let him go!"

Desmond was given his furlough. He and Dorothy were married in a quiet ceremony in Dorothy's church. She came back with him to Fort Jackson. Just knowing she was nearby made military life easier to bear.

# CHAPTER 2

# "...THAT YE MAY BE ABLE TO BEAR IT"

Reveille sounded with a strident urgency one Tuesday morning in late summer. "Come on," roared the sergeants, "get out of those sacks. Today's the day!"

"You don't have to rub it in, Sarge," one of the men in B Company groaned.

They had known it was coming for days. Now it was here. The company was moving out, right after chow, on its first long march. *Twenty-five miles*, with full field pack and a rifle. The march would be completed in eight hours; that meant an average of better than three miles an hour. This was the day that would separate the men from the boys.

"Hey, here's the preacher," one of the riflemen called out as Doss took his place with the 2d Platoon. "How come you didn't get a pass to go to church today?"

"Aw, what's he got to worry about?" another man growled. "No rifle, no ammunition, he's got it made in the shade."

The silent medic grinned, but didn't bother to reply. The two canvas first-aid kits he was carrying were almost as heavy as a rifle and twice as awkward. But he had a feeling he'd be needing the kits before the day was out.

This was more than a physical test for Desmond. It was his first real operation with the men with whom he would go into combat. He was now officially designated as a company aid man, one of the three medical soldiers, or medics, assigned to an infantry company.

For administrative purposes he came under the direction of the medical battalion of the 307th Regiment, but it was the riflemen, the doughboys, the dogfaces, of the 2d Platoon, Company B, 1st Battalion, 307th Infantry, thirty-eight men and one officer, with whom he would go into combat. They would be his medical charges. He would be expected to go to them, even at the risk of his own neck, if they needed him. They should share a close and mutual relationship, he and the men of the 2d Platoon, but in those first days it was just the other way around.

As had been the case with the first company to which he was assigned, the men of Company B were mostly from New York; nearly all were from the North. They were older and tougher, and exuded profanity. They had never known anyone like the soft-voiced young Southerner with his ever-present Bible. They called him "the preacher." They teased him about being married and insisted on dragging Dorothy's name into their earthy remarks about sex. This offended him deeply. He loved Dorothy and knew her to be a Christian woman with high ideals. Their marriage was blessed by God.

The two officers in B Company with whom Doss had contact were Captain Frank L. Vernon, the company commander, and Lieutenant Cecil L. Gornto, 2d Platoon leader. Captain Vernon, a fair and square South Carolinian who gave all he had to the task at hand and expected his men to do likewise, had no time for spare wheels like company aid men. Lieutenant Gornto, an articulate Floridian, was too busy striving to get his platoon up to the high standard of the CO, Captain Vernon, to worry about one medic.

The first sergeant called the company to attention, and turned it over to Captain Vernon. "All right, men," the captain said, in his positive, determined voice, "we've all been training for this for weeks. I expect every man to give it all he's got, and finish this hike on his feet! Platoon leaders, take command of your platoons!"

Lieutenant Gornto, at his place at the head of the 2d Platoon, whipped his hand up to his helmet in a snappy salute. Captain Vernon sang out the orders, the platoon leaders echoing, and B Company swung out of the company area, counting cadence at the top of its collective voice.

Even in the early morning, the summer sun shone hot in the South Carolina sky. The atmosphere was humid. By the time the company had crossed over the first of the rugged little sandy hills, their green cotton fatigues were splotched with sweat. The heat of the day was yet to come and twenty-four miles still lay ahead of them.

By midday the sun beat down like a big broiler in the sky. Some of the men had already drunk a full canteen of water, and now they had no more. They staggered like zombies, their eyes pulled back in red, sweating faces. Suddenly one of the men slumped to his knees and collapsed. Doss hurried to him. It was one of the older fellows, a man in his late thirties. His skin was clammy, his pulse barely perceptible. It was a clear-cut case of heat prostration. Desmond made him as comfortable as possible and turned him over to the ambulance that followed. Then he had to run to catch up with the company.

Captain Vernon, as fresh and tough as he had been when he started, was furious with the soldier for dropping out, and with Doss for not managing somehow to keep him on his feet.

At high noon they took a lunch break—K rations. Desmond had hardly choked down a mouthful when a soldier, slumped under a small tree, called him. The man had his shoe off and was examining a large blister on his heel.

"Can you do anything for this?" he asked.

"I'll sure try," Desmond said. He pricked the blister with a sterile needle, painted it with merthiolate, and then covered it tightly with a gauze dressing. Before he had finished, another man called him. Another, and another, all with the same ailment. While the men of Company B sprawled on their backs, Doss was busy fixing feet. For some severe cases he fashioned a doughnut-shaped pad to relieve the pressure.

It seemed they had been resting only a minute when the first sergeant blew his whistle. "Fall in," he shouted. "It's a long way back."

Blisters and sore feet kept Desmond busy all the way back. He'd fix up a man as best he could, then run to catch up with his platoon. Some of the men he treated weren't even in his company, much less platoon, but they obviously needed help. In spite of all the running he had to do to catch up, his canvas bags flapping at his side, Desmond finished the march with the platoon. Lined up, waiting for dismissal, three men keeled over, out cold. Desmond went to their aid. When he had finished with them, all the other men in the platoon were in their bunks with their shoes off. Desmond did not get a chance even to sit down. He checked every man to see if there was anything he could do to help. That morning some of the men had jeered at him, called him preacher, made derisive remarks. Now, while they lay back exhausted, the slender medic knelt by their bunks and treated their feet.

There was no jeering at Desmond Doss in the barracks that night. He had proved himself. He was one of them now, a fully accepted member of Company B.

As training continued, the three company aid men were drawn closer together. One was Clarence C. Glenn, Jr., a round-faced young man with a big smile which revealed a gold filling in his front tooth. The other aid man was James A. Dorris, also a likable chap but more serious. Both Glenn and Dorris were married, and when Dorothy came to Columbia to be with Desmond, the three couples frequently visited with each other.

Clarence Glenn was the first real live Catholic Desmond had ever known, and Desmond the first Seventh-day Adventist, the first fundamentalist, Glenn had ever been close to. Though some of their comments might have horrified a theologian, still they spent many happy hours discussing their beliefs.

"I just don't see why you make such a fuss about Saturday and Sunday," Glenn said. "Sure, I know what the commandment says, but if practically everybody goes to church on Sunday rather than Saturday, there must be some good reason for it."

"There is a reason, but it's not a good one," Desmond said. "It dates back to the fourth century and a fellow named Constantine. He was a Roman emperor, and a Christian. But most of the Roman subjects those days were pagans, sun worshipers, who observed the sun's day, or Sunday, the first day of the week. Constantine got this great idea that he'd make Sunday a Christian holiday too, and attract all these people. If he couldn't lick 'em, he'd join 'em."

"What happened to Saturday?" Glenn asked.

"Oh, he kept that too," Desmond said.

"You mean he introduced the five-day week," Glenn said with a big grin, his gold tooth flashing.

"Yeah, I guess he did," Desmond agreed, but he didn't smile. He didn't like to make jokes about religion. "Anyhow, they observed both days for, oh, centuries. Originally Saturday was kind of solemn and gradually people began observing Sunday more. Finally the only people who kept the Sabbath were the Jews, just as they'd been doing all along."

"But look, Doss," Glenn objected. In the 77th Division it was always "Doss" and "Glenn"; first names didn't exist. "I just thought of something else. Isn't it hard for you guys to get jobs? I mean, suppose the boss wants you to work Saturday?"

"It's a problem, all right, but we usually find that the Lord works these things out." Desmond paused. How could he tell his friend of his own personal, subjective experience with Sabbath keeping?

From the beginning it was all tied in with the love and inspiration his mother had given him. Being cuddled in her lap, listening to her read and relate stories from the Bible, remained one of his fondest memories.

Desmond's mother had been raised as an Adventist, but his father had not. He smoked and, on occasion, drank. He approved of his wife's religion and found much merit in it, but he put off joining the church himself. One time during the booming twenties Tom Doss asked his employer, a building contractor, whether if he became a Seventh-day Adventist and would no longer work on Saturdays he could keep his job. The boss said No, and that settled the issue for some time.

The Depression came, and virtually no new construction was going on in Lynchburg; Tom Doss was lucky if he could find work any day. Mrs. Doss worked in a shoe factory and the children brought home whatever change they could earn from odd jobs until they were old enough to go to work.

Mrs. Doss and the three children continued to go to church on the Sabbath, and Mr. Doss joined them whenever he could. One Saturday they attended a small church near Lynchburg where Elder Lester Coon was pastor. He was a fiery speaker who said what he believed whether the congregation liked it or not.

In his sermon that Sabbath was one sentence that struck home. He seemed to be looking directly at Tom Doss when he said, "To me any man who doesn't stand up for what he thinks is right is a plain old spaghetti back." Desmond saw his father's back stiffen. For years he had supported his wife and children in their choice of religion; he obviously thought it was right. But he had not stood up for it himself.

Tom Doss joined the church. He quit smoking and drinking. And he was almost immediately put to another test. There had been no work for him for weeks. On Wednesday the boss came to him and asked him to do a small renovation job which would take about two days. He put in Thursday and Friday on the job, but still a few hours' work remained to be done. Doss told the boss frankly that he would not complete the work on the Sabbath; it must wait until Monday. He would not even come in Saturday to get his pay. Then he waited. As far as he knew, the boss might refuse to pay him for the work he had already done.

"That's all right, Tom," the boss said. "Finish it up Monday. Your money will be ready when you finish."

From then on Tom Doss was a devout Adventist and a determined Sabbath keeper. And the strange thing was that from that point on he always had plenty of work Monday through Friday. It was the turning point for the Doss family. "So you see," Desmond told Glenn, winding up the story, "God took care of things in His own way, and it all worked out just right."

"Well, you still do a lot of things I don't want to do," Glenn said. "You really make it rough on yourself. You send ten percent of your paycheck to your church. You wouldn't smoke a cigarette or take a drink if your life depended on it. You won't even eat a pork chop!"

"It's all written in the Bible, yours as well as mine," Desmond said. "Pork is unclean, so is shellfish. I don't know what either one tastes like, so it isn't much of a hardship not to eat them."

"Yeah, but the Bible doesn't say one word about cigarettes or bourbon whiskey."

"Maybe not, but in his first letter to the Corinthians Paul said, 'Ye are the temple of God.' That's what we go on, that the body is the temple of God, and we won't defile the temple with nicotine or alcohol or even coffee or tea. I don't think I'm missing much there, either. I used to smoke corn-silk cigarettes when I was a kid, and sometimes a cigarette butt, but all they did was make me cough. One time I took some cough syrup for a cold and the alcohol in it made me so dizzy I couldn't stand up. Once was enough."

Again Desmond paused. How could he explain to this happy-go-lucky buddy of his that, even if the abstinences did seem harsh, the positive attributes of Adventism made such minor sacrifices worthwhile? He was no gloomy gus; Adventists are a happy group of people. They work toward a goal, a positive, attainable goal, with a reward so great that the imagination can hardly picture it.

For the Adventist also takes literally the word of Christ in the twenty-fourth chapter of Matthew, fourteenth verse: "And this gospel of the kingdom shall be preached in all the world for a witness unto all nations; and then shall the end come."

They interpret this to mean that when the word of the coming of Christ has been made known to everyone, then Christ will come again. The world will end, and the faithful, those who have led Christian lives and made it possible for the gospel to be spread, will live in a heavenly happiness that is absolute, forever. The Adventist has the unmatchable goal of complete security, throughout eternity.

"Isn't that worth a cigarette, or a drink of liquor, or a shrimp cocktail?" Desmond asked. And Glenn smiled his golden smile, punched his buddy lightly on the arm, and suggested they start over to the mess hall for chow.

Out of such discussions grew greater understanding. Another result, of great benefit to the men of Company B, was the arrangement by which Glenn worked Saturdays for Doss so that he could go to church and Doss worked Sundays for Glenn so that he could go to mass. Instead of a reluctant medic on duty against his will, the men of the company found an eager, solicitous young man on hand every day in the week. It became a part of the *esprit de corps* of the company. The men stopped going to the battalion infirmary for minor ailments, preferring to stay with their buddies, confident that their three conscientious medics would take good care of them right there in the company area.

Now the entire division was beginning to pull together as a team. It was shaping up into a fine fighting unit with spirit and pride. It was sent on for further training—to the Louisiana maneuvers for simulated combat conditions, to Arizona for desert training, to Pennsylvania and West Virginia for mountain training.

Dorothy followed Desmond wherever she could. In Louisiana the only place she could find to stay was a dreary room in a dilapidated farmhouse. Another soldier's wife shared the same room. When their husbands could join them, the two couples divided the room by hanging a blanket down the middle.

One Sabbath the division was twenty-five miles from Shreveport, the nearest town. Desmond hitchhiked a ride in with a farmer in an old Ford, but after church he could find no way to get back. Military police picked him up and held him overnight along with a group of drunks and troublemakers. A truck from the regiment picked him up in the stockade next day, and he had to explain to his commanding officer that the only thing he had done wrong was go to church.

By now Major Steinman, commanding the medical battalion, had become so infuriated over the Sabbath issue that he refused to give Desmond his pass to go to church, refused him permission to ask for a pass again, and refused to allow him to go to a higher authority on the matter.

"If you give me the slightest provocation, Doss," the major said, "I'll have you court-martialed."

Desmond knew he meant it. The slightest misstep and he was in trouble. He did not go into town to church that week. Dorothy was staying in the farmhouse nearby, and the two of them went out into a cow pasture and held their own services.

Though Desmond had now earned the respect of the men in B Company, he was still having a hard time with the officers of the medical battalion. Even regimental and division officers got into the hassle. During an important field exercise in which several divisions were involved, Desmond, as usual, asked to be relieved of duties on the Sabbath and to be permitted to go to town to church. The next thing he knew he was told to report to a dusty crossroads in the maneuver area. There, in a command car, were two full colonels, one lieutenant colonel, and a major, all waiting for this one soldier who only wanted to go to church.

It was Lieutenant Colonel Thomas B. Manuel, the regimental executive officer, who did most of the talking. Desmond was respectful and very sorry that these high-ranking officers had to take time away from their important duties to discuss religion with a private. But he was adamant. He wouldn't play war on the Sabbath.

"But I thought you could take care of the sick and the injured on the Sabbath," the colonel said.

"Yes, sir, I believe that it is permissible to do good on the Sabbath, and give medical aid to anyone who needs it," Desmond said. "But colonel, we've run this very same exercise four times now, and nobody's been hurt yet."

Finally the brass gave up and permitted him to go into town and take Dorothy to church.

He hitched a ride with an ambulance, which took him to the camp. It was deserted, except for the guards. Desmond's barracks was locked up tight, except for one window right over his bed. Desmond considered this the result of a direct intervention by God, for surely He would not want His devoted subject to go to young people's meeting sweaty and dirty in fatigues. Desmond carried on God's will by getting a fire ladder and crawling in that unlocked window.

And just then the guard came by. Desmond explained the situation to him from the window.

"Do you need that ladder to get out again?" the guard asked.

"Well, no," Desmond said.

"Then I'm going to put it away before somebody sees it and we both get in trouble," the guard said. "Now you hurry up and get cleaned and dressed and out of here."

Desmond appeared at the meeting that night showered, shaved, and dressed in a fresh uniform. Dorothy was there, waiting for him. Together they gave thanks to the Lord for helping Desmond keep the Sabbath and attend church.

The Division moved to the desert country in Arizona and, after several weeks of maneuvers, settled down far out in the desert. The nearest town was Buckeye, where Dorothy lived in the home of an Adventist doctor and his wife. They had an air-conditioned home, the only comfortable place for miles. Desmond was able to get his Sabbath pass again, but how would he get to town?

A railroad went by, but some soldier-passengers had damaged a train and soldiers were no longer permitted to ride. The only other way to leave camp was by truck across the desert, to Phoenix or Yuma, each a hundred or so miles away. Buckeye was only fifty. Desmond obtained permission from regimental headquarters to ride the train if the railroad would let him. The station agent was perfectly willing to sell a round-trip ticket to this clean-looking young man who wanted only to go to church. And so every Friday, while the other members of the division who had received a pass were jouncing across the desert in trucks, Desmond rode into Buckeye by air-conditioned train and participated in quiet private services with Dorothy and a group of other young people.

Desert training shortened tempers from the top to the bottom. It was a cruel experience that had deleterious effects on the entire division. At that time the United States Army, influenced by operations in the North African desert, was placing extreme emphasis on reducing the amount of water used by the troops. Water, this most common liquid, becomes a precious commodity when it is in short supply. Each unit was severely limited in the amount of water it could have each day. The water was delivered to the company area in fifty-gallon drums in open trucks. Some of the precious stuff would slosh over on the sandy floor of the truck and run out under the tail gate. Men would run after the truck, catch the water in their helmets, and drink it, mud, sand, and all.

On long hikes over the vicious desert, men would fall out through sheer dehydration. Medics were not given extra water, and sometimes Desmond and the others had to share some of their own. Desmond was already severely penalized, for, although his individual consumption was computed in the coffee and tea served at meals, he did not drink these either.

Under such conditions it was easy to get excited about water. One day the men in the company came running to Desmond with the report that Lieutenant Gornto, who was temporarily in command, was making no provision to apportion out the water in the platoon's existing supply. This was a most important procedure. Each morning at a certain time the water trucks would come around to replenish the supply. Kitchen barrels and individual canteens should be filled from what was left in the company water containers before they were refilled. Otherwise they would lose that much water.

"But the lieutenant's just sittin' there doin' nothin'!" the men told Doss excitedly. "We got to get that water!"

Though Doss was only a private, as a medical soldier he had prescribed responsibilities in matters of sanitation and health. He looked into the situation and found out that the men were right. He then felt morally obligated to screw up his courage, approach the lieutenant, and tell him what to do.

Gornto received him casually. He looked tired. "Don't worry about it, Doss," he said. "I'll take care of it."

Doss saluted and left, but still nothing was done. It was now almost time for the trucks to arrive. Doss ran to the headquarters of the medical battalion to report the matter to a medical officer. The officer on duty happened to be a close buddy of Lieutenant Gornto's. Doss felt that the whole thing was an exercise in futility, but again he felt obligated to carry the matter as far as he could.

The medical officer listened to Doss's report. He was obligated to take some action in the matter, and he grudgingly assured Doss that he would do so. By the time Doss returned to the company area, Gornto had had the water distributed. It was a moral victory for Desmond, and the men respected him for it. Gornto never referred to it again, but Desmond was naturally somewhat uneasy with him from then on. It does not make for smooth relations with your platoon leader to blow the whistle on him.

To make the episode still worse, what Doss had not known was that Gornto and his jeep driver, Edward J. Panek, had spent most of the night looking for the water truck. Gornto had known all along that it would be later than usual.

The men of the 77th existed in an atmosphere of parched heat, irritability, misunderstanding, and distrust. Conditions were so miserable that desertion was common. Some men fled into the desert and were never seen again. Even one of the chaplains went AWOL! Only in such an environment could the next episode in Private Doss's war with the Army have taken place. Going into the hot headquarters tent of the medical battalion to pick up his pass one Friday, he noticed that the chair-borne commandos, the pencil pushers, were giving each other knowing looks. The top sergeant, who reflected with magnification the commanding officer's disapproval of Doss, handed over the pass with an unpleasant grin.

"I won't be doing this much longer, Doss," he said. "Arrangements are being made so that you can have all your Saturdays off from now on."

Something was in the wind, Desmond knew. He went to one of the officers of the battalion to find out what was going on.

"I've got good news for you, Private Doss," he said. "You're getting out of the Army. We've discussed your case at length and have come to the conclusion that you are eligible for discharge under the terms of Section

Eight. You'll appear before the discharge committee this morning. Go to your tent. You'll be summoned when they're ready for you."

Desmond's spirits went up—then down. He was human, and he had had enough of this desert. His nose was swollen and inflamed from the constant dust; his eyes were watering. The officers were down on him; he could never relax. He'd had enough. He was ready to go home.

But "Section Eight," he knew, referred to mental instability. And Desmond Doss did not believe that, just because he wanted to go to church on Saturday, he was a nut.

The discharge committee, composed of five medical officers, sat around a folding table out in the open. The papers were already made out. The chairman told Desmond what he already knew, that he was up for discharge.

"Why Section Eight?" he stammered. He was one lone private facing five military doctors who thought he was crazy. What could he say? "Hasn't my work been satisfactory?"

"Well, yes, it has," the chairman admitted. "But everyone else in this unit is training seven days a week. Your refusal to train with the rest of the men on Saturdays means that you are missing valuable training. You can miss something important which could keep you from doing your job properly. A man's life could be at stake. Even your own life could be in danger."

Desmond pointed out how he and Clarence Glenn had worked out an efficient system by which one of them was on duty during the weekend, and that Company B had the lowest number of men on sick call in the regiment. Committee members might as well not have heard him. Obviously they wanted him to agree to accept the discharge without protest. But this he could not do.

"You say my work is satisfactory," he said, "so the only grounds you have for my discharge is my keeping the Sabbath. I'd be a very poor Christian to accept a discharge implying that I was mentally off purely because of my religion. When I'm called upon to treat my fellow soldiers on the Sabbath, I will do it, and willingly. I don't believe that I am missing anything of importance by not being here on Saturdays, but if I do miss anything, even something that might endanger my life, well, I'll just take that chance."

Desmond paused for breath. "Sir," he said softly, "please believe me. I know that if I keep God's commandments, He will give me wisdom and understanding equal to those who receive training on His holy day."

That answer stopped the Section Eight discharge, right there. It was obvious that Washington would never approve a discharge given on purely religious grounds. Desmond remained in the Army, on the desert—a strange victory. His situation was even worse than before, for it was all over the division that the officers of the medical battalion had tried to railroad a good soldier out of the Army, and had gotten themselves chewed out instead. This did not increase Desmond's popularity with the brass.

Finally, now, this desert training hell was coming to a close. Word came down that the division's next stop would be the Indiantown Gap Military Reservation in Pennsylvania. Trees, grass, plenty of water, and no more sand. Elation swept through the entire division.

At noon Desmond Doss came in from the field, hot and dry but happy in the knowledge that soon this would end. Waiting for him was an order to report to regimental headquarters. And there he was told that he had been officially transferred out of the medics, into the headquarters company of the regiment. He was in the infantry again. His enemies in the medical battalion had gotten rid of him in another way.

In a kind of daze, Desmond went to his tent to get his medical equipment and turn it in. Then he would report to his new company. He couldn't find a strap. Suddenly he realized that that one piece of canvas was all that stood between him and the infantry, that now his troubles were really beginning. He fell on his knees.

"Help me, O Lord," he begged. "Give me wisdom so that I will know what to do."

He remembered Captain Stanley, who had helped him before. The missing strap gave him time to visit the chaplain, but Captain Stanley could give him only sympathy and good wishes. Finally Desmond found the strap and, knowing he was in for trouble, turned in his equipment. One of his friends, T/4 March Howell, told him good-bye.

"And say, Doss," Howell added, "I just made a ten-dollar bet with your new company commander. He said he'd have you carrying a gun in thirty days. I bet you wouldn't."

"You know I don't approve of gambling, sergeant," Desmond said. "I don't want either one of you to lose. But I'm not going to carry a gun."

Desmond reported to his new company commander, Lieutenant Walter G. Cosner.[3] The lieutenant had been primed that a troublemaker was being transferred to his platoon, and he was ready for him. Doss was

---

3    A pseudonym.

already assigned to the pioneer ammunition section, and the carbine he was to carry was waiting for him.

"Private Doss," the lieutenant said, "take this carbine."

Desmond instantly realized the cat-and-mouse game the lieutenant was playing with him. Though as a conscientious objector he was officially exempt from bearing arms, no soldier is exempt from the obligation to obey the direct command of a commissioned officer. The lieutenant was out to make him either take the weapon or be court-martialed.

"I'm sorry, sir," Doss said, "but according to my religious convictions, I cannot bear arms."

Again the lieutenant ordered Doss to take the rifle, and again Doss declined, phrasing his answer in such a way that it was not a direct refusal.

The lieutenant tired of playing games with the rifle, and picked up a .45 automatic pistol. "You can take this, Doss," he said. "This isn't really a weapon."

"Then what is it, sir?" Doss asked. The lieutenant played the game with a trench knife, then an ammunition kit. Doss declined both, again without making a direct refusal.

"Look, Doss," the lieutenant said, "I don't want you to kill anybody. I just want you to train with these weapons, like everybody else."

"I would rather put my faith in the Lord than confidence in a carbine," Desmond said.

The lieutenant leaned forward. "You're married. Now suppose somebody was raping your wife. Wouldn't you use a gun?"

"I wouldn't have one."

"What would you do, then?"

"I wouldn't just stand there," Doss said sharply. "I wouldn't use a gun, and I wouldn't kill, but he'd sure wish he was dead when I got through with him."

The conflict was interrupted by the move to Indiantown Gap. There the lieutenant had the last word. Doss was placed on permanent KP and given the job of scrubbing the pots and pans. The unrelieved exposure to the harsh lye in the soap left his hands raw and bleeding. He was refused a pass to leave the company area, which meant that it would be useless for Dorothy to come to Indiantown Gap.

A telegram arrived from home. His younger brother Harold was home on his last furlough before going overseas with the Navy. This would be the last chance for the whole family to be together. About this time several men in the platoon, including Doss, became eligible for a furlough and they all put in for it. The lieutenant had the papers prepared and lined up the men, presenting each one with his papers. When he came to Doss he placed the papers in his outstretched hand.

"You haven't qualified with your weapon yet, have you, Doss?" he asked. "Well, there's a regulation that no man gets his furlough until he does."

He snatched the papers back and tore them up.

Desmond went to the chaplain and all the way to the colonel of the regiment, but both told him there was nothing they could do. Sadly he walked over to the telephone in the Post Exchange and called his family long distance.

"I can't come home," he said. Then he choked up. He was in serious trouble. He might never see his brother again. He might never see any of his loved ones again. The way things were going, he could wind up in prison. He stood there clutching the phone, unable to speak, as the seconds he was paying for ticked by.

"Desmond," his mother was crying. "Desmond! What's the matter? Where are you? Desmond!"

Finally he controlled himself and poured out the whole story.

Next morning Desmond was up to his elbows in lye soap when he got word to report to the medical battalion. Major Steinman was waiting for him. "Welcome back," he said.

The top sergeant said, "Go report to your old company. You're back in the medics."

"Can I have a furlough?" Desmond asked, and explained his home situation. In any event, he was due a furlough.

But things had not changed. Desmond would have to wait for a furlough. He could have a three-day pass—in which case, no furlough.

"I'll take the pass," Desmond sighed.

He started for home immediately. When he arrived he found out what had happened. His father had gotten in touch with Carlyle B. Haynes, chairman of the church's War Service Commission in Washington. Haynes called the regimental commander, Colonel Stephen S. Hamilton. "I understand you're having some difficulty up there, colonel," he had said pleasantly. "Is it necessary for me to come there and look into it?"

"Oh, no, not at all," the colonel said. "Whatever it is, we can straighten it out right here."

Desmond had been transferred back to the medics immediately after. However, just in case, Haynes sent to both the regimental commander and to Doss copies of documents signed by both President Roosevelt, commander in chief, and General George C. Marshall, chief of staff, affirming that conscientious objectors would not have to bear arms.

With Desmond now definitely in the medical battalion, 307th Regiment, assigned to Company B, the division continued training, at Indiantown Gap, a West Virginia training area, and at Camp Pickett, Virginia. Doss's unit drove up into the West Virginia mountains in open trucks wearing khakis, and into seven inches of snow.

While they trained in the mountains there, a minor episode occurred which was to assume great importance later, in combat. Several training periods were given over to learning how to tie knots which would be useful in mountain climbing. Through his membership in the Junior Missionary Volunteers, Desmond was thoroughly familiar with the knots, but he pitched in and practiced just the same. One day there was a shortage of rope and Doss did not have one to practice on. Two men were sharing one long rope, one at each end, and Desmond took the middle part, doubled it, and practiced with that. When he tied a bowline, a loop that will not slip, in the doubled line, he found that he had two loops rather than one. Both held securely. He had never seen this done before and he tucked it away in his mind.

In the second week of March 1944, the 77th Division made its last move in the United States. Well trained, at full strength, with good morale and determined to prove themselves in battle, the men of the Statue of Liberty Division boarded special troop trains at Camp Pickett and headed west toward the Pacific and the Japanese. Dorothy, along with many other wives, was permitted to come to the company area to say good-bye. She and Desmond had said their good-byes in the privacy of the camp guesthouse the night before. Now they could only look into each other's eyes and repeat again, "I love you, I love you."

The next major city to the west was Lynchburg. Desmond was on KP, peeling potatoes in a baggage car, when he began to recognize landmarks on the outskirts of his hometown. He knew that the train would pass close to the Doss home. He also knew that his father liked to watch the trains go by. Desmond called the other men on KP with him, and they all got mops and brooms and stationed themselves in the open double doors. Sure enough, there was the familiar house and the familiar figure on the front porch.

"OK, now!" Desmond hollered, and his buddies began waving their mops and brooms. Mr. Doss waved back, with no idea that he was waving to his own son.

On the spur of the moment Desmond took a paper napkin and hastily wrote on it, "Dear Mom and Dad, I'm on the way. Pray for me."

He tied a handkerchief around the paper, wrote his parent's name and address on the outside, and threw it off the train in hopes it would be found and taken to his parents. (It was, the next day.)

The train rattled on through Lynchburg, over a high trestle, toward the Pacific. Desmond looked longingly back toward the scenes of his childhood. Two good-byes in one day would take a lot out of any soldier. His spirits, already low, suddenly hit bottom. He had the sudden fear that he would never see his loved ones again. The train was still crossing over the trestle. *I might as well jump off,* he thought disconsolately.

Instead, Desmond reached in his pocket and pulled out his most precious possession. It was the Bible Dorothy had given him after they were married. In it she had marked a truly appropriate verse, 1 Corinthians 10:13, for encouragement. He read it again: "There hath no temptation taken you but such as is common to man: but God is faithful, who will not suffer you to be tempted above that ye are able; but will with the temptation also make a way to escape, that ye may be able to bear it."

Then he turned to the first page. There was a letter she had written in the Bible before presenting it to him. As the train carried him westward, each click of the wheels beneath him taking him farther and farther away from the woman he loved, Desmond read, as he had so many times before, the words she had written.

*November 22, 1942*

*Dearest Desmond,*

*As you read and study the precious promises found in the word of God contained in this little Bible, may you be strengthened in whatever trials may come to you.*

*May your faith in God bring comfort and peace of heart to you, that you may never be sad or lonely no matter how dark the way seems.*

*If we do not meet another time on this earth, we have the assurance of a happy meeting place in heaven. May God in His mercy grant us both a place there.*

*Your loving wife,*
*Dorothy*

Desmond Doss closed the Bible and put it back in his pocket over his heart. What a wonderful letter. Once again he drew courage and comfort from it. He sighed and, as the train picked up speed, he went back to his potatoes. And so he was off to war.

# CHAPTER 3

## COMBAT!

A heavy sea was running and the big transport ship pitched and rolled like a crazy sea monster. At her side, but far beneath, the landing craft bobbed and wallowed erratically in the gray-green Pacific. A driving rain beat against the ponchos, helmets, and unprotected faces of the men. It obscured the distant shoreline, and the howling wind muffled the sounds of artillery fire and exploding shells.

"OK, Second Platoon, start loading!" Lieutenant Willis A. J. Munger,

American troops offloading landing craft on an unidentified beachhead in the South Pacific. Desmond participated in three similar landings: Leyte, Philippines, Guam and Okinawa. (Courtesy Del E. Webb Memorial Library, Loma Linda University, California.)

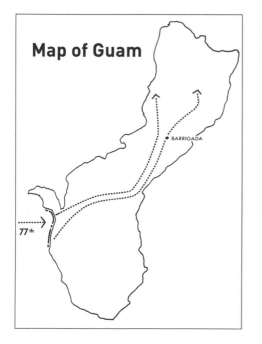

**Map of Guam**

BARRIGADA

77th

American soldiers take defensive positions on an unknown beachhead in a South Pacific campaign. This picture, along with a few similar photographs, was found among Desmond's personal papers after his death. It is conceivable that it is a photo of one of the three landings in which he took part: Leyte, Guam or Okinawa. (Courtesy Del E. Webb Memorial Library, Loma Linda University, California.)

Litter bearers evacuate a wounded soldier to relative safety and a medical aid station inland after a beach landing in the South Pacific. (Courtesy Del E. Webb Memorial Library, Loma Linda University, California.)

United States troops of the 77th
Division move up to front lines,
Guam. (U.S. Army photo.)

Scene at a battalion aid station, Guam. This
is the first stop for the wounded brought
back from the front (U.S. Army photo).

American troops, returning
to Guam to recapture the
island previously lost to
Japanese, wade ashore from
landing craft to White Beach
area (U.S. Army photo).

the fresh-faced young officer who was replacing Lieutenant Gornto temporarily, slung his leg over the rail. The other men followed. Now it was Doss's turn. On his back was his field pack, his canteen and shovel on his belt. From each shoulder hung a big canvas first-aid kit. Carrying more than seventy-five pounds, the driving rain beating into his face, his cold, wet hands clutching the rail, the ship bucking and rearing, he felt with his feet for the thick rope of the landing net slung on the side of the ship. He found a foothold and began the long climb down to the landing craft.

Crosses in Agat Cemetery testify to heavy casualties
in invasion of Guam (U.S. Army photo).

Explosive charges burst inside an enemy dugout
on Rota Peninsula, Guam (U.S. Army photo).

"All aboard, sir!" a voice shouted.

"Cast off!"

The boat slowly moved away from the parent ship and headed toward the rendezvous point, pitching and tossing in the waves. Now up, with a swoosh, now down with a sickening lift in the pit of the stomach.

It wasn't long before nausea gripped even the toughest men. Lieutenant Munger, younger than most of the men he commanded, tried to keep his dignity, but his face was turning green.

Wretched and miserable in the open boat in the driving rain, Desmond Doss and his 2d Platoon proceeded to their first action. It was a dramatic, daring operation. If successful, it would extend the American spearhead a full thousand miles deep into the Japanese-held island area between Japan itself and the Caroline Islands. The 77th's objective was Guam, largest of the Marianas and an American possession which the Japanese had taken shortly after Pearl Harbor.

Ever since the arrival in Hawaii on April 1, 1944, two years to the day after Desmond's induction, the 77th had been training for this operation, the assault on a fortified island. Part of the preparation had involved the arming of all medical soldiers. Tragic experience had shown the American army that the Japanese were instructed to seek out and kill medical soldiers in the correct assumption that it would affect morale. The battalion executive officer, Colonel Gerald G. Cooney, had ordered Doss to carry a weapon, and on his refusal, had recommended that he be returned to the States. Captain Vernon, B Company's CO, had interceded at the last moment, and Desmond remained with the company.

Now, approaching Guam, Desmond was not so sure that staying had been a good idea. It was an actual relief when the LCI scraped the coral reef some 400 yards from the beach. The ramp was lowered, and one of the men gingerly dropped himself into the water. It was up to his chin. Doss went in up to his armpits. Some of the shorter men, weighed down with pack, rifle, and ammunition, had to be helped on the long, sloshing walk to shore.

Weakened by nausea, exhausted after wading a quarter of a mile, the men of B Company assembled on the beach. The American soldiers who had fallen on the first assault had been removed, but Japanese bodies lay everywhere. They lay in twisted positions, on front and back, in and out of mudholes. Desmond tried not to look at the bodies. The Army had tried to teach him to hate the enemy, but it had not been successful.

Desmond checked with his buddies, Glenn and Dorris. They had reached shore safely. With Captain Vernon at the head, the company

1st Battalion, 307th Infantry Regiment, assembled for a formal picture circa 1942 and prior to embarkation for the South Pacific. Included are members from the 307th Medical Detachment. Pvt. Desmond Doss can be seen in the back row, seventh from the left, to the right of the chimney in the background.

started a five-mile hike to their bivouac area. Under the combination of heavy tanks and the tropical downpour, the trail was a series of mudholes, some waist deep. When they reached the area, the men were at the limit of their endurance. Desmond opened his package of K-rations. It contained a chunk of cheese with bacon in it. As he could not eat pork, he gave it away to those who could and started munching on the hard, tasteless crackers that came in the package. The GIs called them dog biscuits. The K-ration package also contained cigarettes and coffee. Not approving of either, Desmond threw them both away—a moral luxury that would not last too many days. They could be traded for another dog biscuit or a candy bar.

The first battalion of the 307th Infantry, which included Company B, was being held in reserve, and for four days the cold, wet soldiers sat huddled in their ponchos by day, shivered in holes that had to be constantly bailed out by night. Their uniforms, green cotton fatigues, never dried out. Their feet were always wet.

Then came orders to move out, and to move out fast. The mission was to cross the narrow island to the east, then drive northward to the crossroads of Barrigada. This was a vital point. A functioning well was located there. In spite of all that rain, the invasion forces were running out of water. There were few wells on this coral island. Barrigada had to be taken.

It was about eight miles across the island, another five up to Barrigada. These are crow's-flight distances; the actual mileage, around hills and over winding jungle trails, was much further. Nor was the terrain secure. In the haste to get water, the forward elements were driving straight through, bypassing Japanese snipers, rearguard patrols, and even large pockets of the enemy. The battalion traveled as a self-contained unit. As it passed through, the jungle closed up after it. There was nobody behind.

Desmond chose his position at about two-thirds back from the head of the platoon. It would be pointless for him to march at the front, not only because he was a high-priority target, but because he could not watch his men from there. But it would also be unwise to bring up the rear.

They pushed along briskly. An occasional sniper's bullet whistled by, but no one in the platoon was injured. The men watched where they put their feet, and were careful to touch nothing. They had been warned against booby traps. The Japanese even booby-trapped their own dead. Roll a corpse over, and a grenade would go off.

But of course no Japanese would drop an American fountain pen. One of the men saw it, lying bright and shiny by the trail. He was a happy-go-lucky, impulsive kid.

"Hey, look at that," he cried, "a fountain pen!"

Three of the men who were near him stopped and joined him as he picked it up. Suddenly an explosion shook the jungle. The pen had triggered a white phosphorus grenade.

Desmond heard the cry—"Medic! Doss! Doss!" He hurried forward. He smelled the burning flesh before he reached the men; white phosphorus sticks to the skin as it burns with a white heat. The man who had picked up the pen had taken most of the blast. His torso was a bloody mess. The other men were suffering from severe burns and wounds caused by pieces of flying metal.

Desmond slung off his first-aid kits and went to work. The man who had activated the booby trap was in the worst shape. He had lost a lot of blood, was critically burned, and was already in a state of shock. Desmond stanched the flow of blood and treated the burns. Another man was also in bad shape. Desmond treated him next. The other two were better off. By the time he had finished, four litter bearers had come up. They would carry the two seriously injured men back to the battalion aid station; the other two were classified as walking wounded and traveled under their own power.

Not until it was over did Desmond realize that he had treated his first casualties. He had not panicked. If the two badly injured men lived, it would be because of his prompt, efficient action. Before starting after his unit, Desmond paused to give thanks to the Lord for enabling him to do his job.

Desmond caught up with the 2d Platoon before nightfall. They were getting close to the main Japanese forces now, passing abandoned equipment and bivouac areas where the fires were still warm. That night seven Japanese were killed trying to infiltrate the company area.

There had been no official water for days, and the men had gotten what they could where they could. As a result nearly everyone suffered from nausea, headaches, and diarrhea. They could appreciate the need to capture Barrigada.

The battle order came down. The 2d Platoon was in the very center of the battalion front, headed on a crossroads. They dashed through the jungle. Suddenly Pfc Julian R. Perez, the platoon scout, started firing. A light machine gun opened up. Pfc Angelo B. Pacella went down. Lieutenant Munger halted the advance and sent a group of men around on each side to envelope the machine gun. They knocked it out, and the advance continued.

The battle grew hotter. Several companies were now involved, all of them blasting away. The Japanese returned the fire. Doss scooped out a little hole and made himself as small as possible. Down the road he saw a green-clad American soldier jump up and start running forward in a crouching position. Suddenly he went down and lay motionless. Out of nowhere an officer, obviously the fallen soldier's company commander, came running, standing straight up, waving his hands and shouting the man's name.

Desmond began running toward him too, but he kept low. The soldier was lying on his face where he had fallen. Desmond crossed one of the soldier's legs over the other and turned him so that he lay face up. Blood was all over the man's chest. His captain looked on helplessly. Desmond took both hands and ripped the fatigue jacket open. A shell fragment had torn a big hole in the victim's chest.

The medic knew there was little he could do, but he opened up his kit and took out a large battle dressing just the same. As he was putting it in place, the soldier let out his last breath. He was dead.

Desmond breathed one short, quick, but fervent prayer, then he and the captain sped back toward cover. Not until after Desmond had dived into the jungle underbrush and gasped for breath did he realize that he had just lost his first American soldier.

In front of Barrigada lay a large clearing. On the other side stood a deserted green shack. "That looks like good protection," Munger said. "Let's take it."

Munger and Perez, crouching low and zigzagging, ran across the field to the shack. The other men of the platoon, in groups of twos and threes, followed. Suddenly an enemy tank, the machine gun on its turret hammering out fire and death, came through the village and roared up to the regimental command post, leaving wounded and dead men in its wake. Two men from the 2d Platoon had been hit. The Japanese started pasting the green shack with mortar and artillery.

"Anyone who wants to go can leave—I wouldn't blame you," Munger told his men. "But I'm sticking."

The men stuck with him. Sergeant Charles J. Kunze volunteered to go for reinforcements. He dashed across the open field and reported the situation to Captain Vernon.

"Tell Munger to come back," Vernon said. "That shack isn't worth it."

Kunze dashed across the field again, delivered the message. As other members of the company, under fire, covered them, Munger led his men out of the shack. He was hit and fell—dead. Perez and Kunze were wounded. But the Japanese attack was beaten off. The next morning the village was taken, along with the well and a small reservoir of water.

After the Americans secured the village, they collected the dead and placed them together. Some of the native Chamorros had also lost their lives in the battle. Desmond was walking near the collection area when he heard a slight moan. He thought he saw one of the natives stir. These people had been of great help to the Americans. Desmond went to the man and knelt by his side. He could feel no pulse. He placed his finger gently on the carotid artery in the neck. There was the slightest sensation of movement. The man was still alive!

Desmond examined him, found the wound, and treated it. He then checked all the bodies. Another, an American, was also alive. Desmond had both men taken to the battalion aid station. From then on he never gave up on any man until positive he was dead.

"Haven't you got enough to do, taking care of our own men?" Glenn asked. "Why try to resurrect these natives?"

"Because it's not up to me to judge whether one of God's children should live or die," Desmond said. "That is a decision for the Lord to make, not me. I believe that I should do everything in my power to help all men hold on to life."

"Suppose they aren't fit to live?"

"Well, the way I look at it," Desmond said, "is that anybody who isn't fit to live surely isn't fit to die! What worse fate could possibly happen to any mortal than to die when he doesn't deserve to live? That would seal his doom forever. No matter how evil a person may be he deserves to live, for he may discover the teachings of Jesus and be saved!"

At Barrigada the 307th lost eighty-five men killed and wounded. The miserable conditions—constant rain, polluted water, clouds of flies and mosquitoes—also took their toll in sickness.

But the push against the Japanese continued. Patrols constantly probed ahead of the advancing line. If they found no resistance, the larger bodies of troops moved up. If they met resistance, then the decision had to be made by higher echelons when to attack and in what strength.

Whenever the 2d Platoon was assigned a patrol mission, Desmond went along with his men. His old friend Sergeant Howell, one of the senior noncoms at the battalion aid station, heard that Desmond was going out on patrol with the dogfaces.

"Have you lost your mind, Doss?" he demanded. "It's not your job to get killed. Your job is to stay alive so that you can help these men when they get hit. If Captain Vernon or anybody else tries to send you on patrol you tell him it's not your duty."

"It may not be my duty," Desmond told him, "but it's what I believe in. I know these men; they're my buddies. They have families, some have wives and children. If they're hurt I want to be there to take care of them."

He continued to go out on patrol, slipping noiselessly through the jungles, maintaining constant visual contact with the men in front of him, peering about for any suspicious activity, ever alert to the danger of booby traps and mines. If the patrol was fired upon and a man was hit, the other men would close in and cover Doss while he administered first aid. Then they'd all retreat together, helping the wounded man to safety.

Even when they encountered no opposition, the patrols were more efficient with Doss along. He gave the men confidence. Even the bravest soldier has a horror of being wounded and left behind, helpless, at the mercy of the enemy. For the enemy had no mercy. But with Doss along that fear was alleviated, for they knew their medic wouldn't leave them.

Captain Vernon and the other officers came to expect Doss to go out with the men. Vernon himself, as brave and as fair as any officer in the Army, went out himself, and he expected no less of any of his men.

And yet friction developed between the brave captain and the brave medic. When a man received a slight wound that might become infected, when he was so sick with fever or diarrhea that he couldn't do his job, Doss insisted that he return to the battalion aid station to be checked by a medical officer. Sometimes the man did not return. Captain Vernon felt that Doss was oversolicitous. He himself would fight on as long as he was conscious, and he expected his men to do the same.

"That man wasn't badly hurt," he raged at Doss one day. "You didn't have to send him back."

"He needed more attention than I could give him, captain," Doss said quietly. "I didn't have any choice."

"You pill rollers are mollycoddling these men," Vernon said. "We're fighting a war up here, not running a hospital."

"Captain," Doss said, "some of these men are so sick they couldn't do you or themselves any good. On patrol they don't know what they're doing. They'll get themselves and the rest of us killed."

In the meantime, pressure was coming on him from another direction. "What's this I hear about you going out on patrols?" Captain Leo Tann, the medical officer at the battalion aid station, said. "You can't do anybody any good if you get shot yourself. Leave the patrols to the riflemen. You stay in the company area where you belong."

Desmond had been at the aid station picking up supplies. When he returned to the company, he found that his platoon had been moved out. He set out through the jungle, trying to overtake them, but he had gone only a couple of hundred yards when another officer in the company saw him.

"Get back, Doss," he said. "There are Japanese all through here."

"But I'm trying to find my platoon," Doss said.

"They're way up ahead now," the officer said. "You'd never make it alive. Get back! That's an order."

Back at the company area, Desmond had a feeling of unease, as though something was going to happen. That night he uttered a special prayer to the Lord for his men. He had never failed to say his daily prayers, incidentally, morning and evening. He even returned thanks when he munched dog biscuits and washed them down with foul-tasting water. But he no longer knelt at all times. On the front there was constant danger of Japanese infiltrating past the company perimeter. Standing orders were to shoot at anything that moved. If Desmond had stuck his head out of his hole he would likely have gotten it shot off. And so, he reasoned, God would hear his prayers whether he was standing, kneeling, or lying shivering in a muddy hole.

That night he asked the Lord that, if it were His will, He give special protection to the men of the 2d Platoon. In the morning Lieutenant George M. Black, who had replaced Lieutenant Munger, burst into the company area with two of his men. All three had been slightly wounded.

"An artillery and mortar barrage zeroed in on us and kept it up all night," Black reported. "Several of our men were hit. They need attention."

Desmond threw his first-aid kits over his shoulders. "I'm ready, sir," he said.

The lieutenant led the medic and a squad of riflemen back to the platoon. Snipers fired on them all the way. Several men were injured and Desmond dressed their wounds. From their description of the barrage, he knew that it was a miracle that any man had lived. Yet of the entire platoon, only one man lost his life. When he had treated the last wounded man, Desmond Doss bowed his head and humbly gave thanks to the Lord for hearing his prayer.

On the way back he was twice as vulnerable to the snipers' bullets, for now he was helping one of his men who hobbled with a leg wound. The two made their way through the jungle with the wounded man hopping on one leg, his arm around Desmond's neck for support. A dozen times bullets whistled through the foliage, and the two dropped to the ground. It was a long trip and a painful one, but they reached the company area safely.

Two days later the company was together again. Again a 2d Platoon patrol went out, this time without their medic. When Captain Vernon learned that Desmond had not accompanied the patrol, he told him to catch up with it. By that time the patrol was deep in the woods. Japanese snipers were all through that area. Even more dangerous, Doss knew, were the green replacements in the patrol. They'd shoot at anything.

"It's too late to go now, captain," Desmond said. "If the Japanese don't get me the new men will."

"Do you refuse to go?" Vernon demanded.

"Captain, I'd just get myself killed, and I'm under orders not to take that kind of chance."

Vernon blew up. "I'm going to have you court-martialed!" he shouted. "You chancre mechanics have to take orders like everybody else."

Desmond hurried to the battalion aid station to report the situation to Captain Tann. The medical officer in turn immediately made a report to regimental headquarters. Tann had heard of Vernon's references to his medics as pill rollers and chancre mechanics and was annoyed with him. There was no court-martial, and Captain Vernon was officially informed that Doss took orders from the medical battalion, not the officers of B Company. The episode officially closed, but Desmond knew it had rankled the captain.

Desmond himself, about this time, learned something about the responsibility of command. The battalion was cleaning up sporadic resistance north of Barrigada. It moved swiftly, as a self-contained unit. The jungle closed up behind it as it passed.

Suddenly shots rang out. Ambush! Four men were seriously wounded. Desmond got to them first and gave them emergency treatment.

By now nearly all the battalion had gone by. What would Desmond do with the wounded men? They could not walk, and he couldn't leave them there. While he worked on them some men came by with litters and dropped four. Then came the rear guard. After that there was nobody except perhaps the Japanese. The rear guard was under the command of an infantry sergeant. Desmond didn't know him, but he knew the sergeant would have to be tough and competent to be entrusted with so critical an assignment.

"I need some of your men to carry these wounded," Doss told him.

"Are you crazy? This is the rear guard. I can't spare any men."

"You've got to. Do you think I'm going to leave these men here to die?"

"I can't help that," the sergeant snapped. "All I know is I can't leave any men."

He was shouting, and Desmond shouted right back. "I'm a medical soldier, and this is an emergency and I'm ordering you to help me carry these wounded American soldiers. And if you don't I'm going to get your name and serial number and you'll be busted right down to a private."

"Well, I've got to ask the lieutenant. He's gone on."

"OK, then, go ask," Desmond agreed, "but leave some men here until you come back."

The sergeant started running up the trail after the lieutenant. The jungle became quiet. There was only a handful of men and the wounded, and they all kept looking about apprehensively. But the sergeant came running back.

"All right," the sergeant panted, "the lieutenant says take what you need, but make it snappy. Let's get out of here."

Four men quickly grabbed the handles of each litter and set off at a quick step along the trail. Desmond stuck with them until he could transfer the casualties, all still alive, to the rear.

---

The campaign on Guam was drawing to a close. Only mopping-up operations remained. The 77th Division moved into a bivouac area for a rest and to break in the new replacements. And Captain Tann summoned Desmond to the aid station.

"I'm having you transferred out of Company B," he said. "You'll be a litter bearer working out of this aid station. If Captain Vernon doesn't know what to do with the best company aid man in the Army, well, I do."

Desmond packed up his things and moved in with the medical battalion. He had several friends there. One of them was a litter bearer named Herbert Schechter. Herb was a short, chunky fellow with black curly hair. He was quiet, sincere, and religious. Like Desmond, he observed the Sabbath, but as a Jew, not an Adventist. The two young men liked to discuss religion, finding pleasure in their close agreement on many philosophical points.

"Boy, am I glad to see you!" Herb cried. "I'll bet you're not sorry to be out of that outfit."

"No, I guess not," Desmond said. But deep inside he wasn't so sure. Up there with the fighting men he felt he could best serve his fellow men and his country, and therefore his God. Perhaps it was where he belonged.

# CHAPTER 4

## "PRAY FOR ME, DOSS"

Nothing is so restful as a tropical ocean cruise, and during most of the month of November 1944, the combat-weary men of the 77th Division lazed their way through long, uneventful days and tropical, star-filled nights. As the big transport plowed on smoothly southward toward the rest area on New Caledonia, Desmond liked to get out of the smoky bowels of the ship at night and lie on the deck in the balmy equatorial climate, the bright stars just out of reach above him.

For the first time in months the men had plenty of good fresh food to eat, and Doss felt the strength come back into his weary muscles.

During the day he caught up on his Bible course, "Brief Bible Studies for Busy People." He had been studying his Bible for as long as he could remember, and he welcomed the opportunity to spend hours a day with this reliable old friend. This was the Bible Dorothy had given him, and often he would turn to that letter she had written. Though she was a third of a world away, the opening salutation, *Dearest Desmond,* written in her beloved, familiar hand, made her seem closer.

As he studied his Bible, other men frequently came up and discussed religion with him. Desmond had written out many of the answers to the most common questions asked of him on small pieces of paper and had tucked them in the appropriate places in the Bible. He could turn to the proper place, flick his eye over what he had written, and give the correct answer almost instantaneously. The word passed all over the ship that here was a man who really knew his Bible.

A passage he found strangely heartening was the prophecy of "wars and rumors of wars" and other dire events in Matthew, chapter 24. With other Adventists he interpreted this to mean that after this period of world calamity Christ will come again. Not everyone agreed with him that the war was really a fine omen, however.

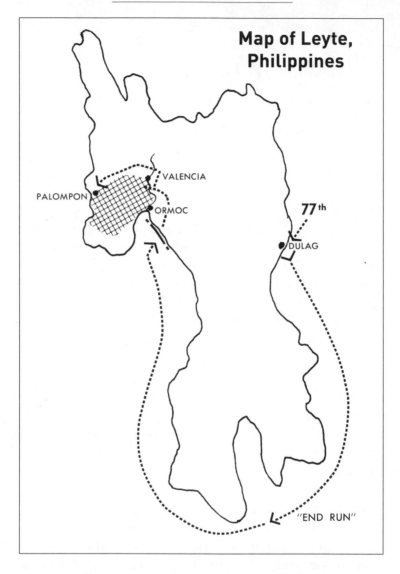

Map of Leyte, Philippines

Mostly, of course, Desmond talked with his old buddies, Glenn and Dorris and Herb Schechter. But frequently other men would come and discuss theology with him. One of the officers of B Company, Lieutenant Kenneth Phillips, a devout Presbyterian from North Carolina, also liked to talk religion. Desmond did not see much of the other officers. Captain Vernon remained especially aloof, and most of the other officers of B Company followed his lead.

Desmond missed the close camaraderie he had enjoyed with the men of the 2d Platoon and B Company, but he saw no point in crying over it. He would continue to do his best to serve his God and his fellow man and his country and hope that everything would work out all right.

Four days out of New Caledonia the convoy suddenly made a sweeping turn and headed toward the northwest. Within minutes the news was all over Desmond's transport: there would be no rest on New Caledonia for the weary men of the 77th. The division was heading for the island of Leyte in the Philippines.

The news came as no great surprise. Broadcasts picked up by the ship's radio told how the American advance had slowed down on Leyte. The Japanese high command had publicly stated its intention to make the Leyte campaign the decisive one of the Philippine Islands. The Japanese were putting everything they had on this small strategic island south of Luzon.

On the way north the convoy stopped in at the island of Manus to pick up replacements and supplies. Then on to the east coast of Leyte, where the division landed on an already secured beachhead. This was now the rainy season, with water everywhere—in the sky, in the air, on the ground. The rice paddies were all flooded, knee-deep in muddy water, and the roads were not much better. Dry feet became an almost impossible luxury.

Two weeks after landing on Leyte, the troops were hastily recalled in great secrecy, loaded on board transports again, and taken around the southern tip of the island. When the transports put to sea, officers and men were gathered into groups over the ship and briefed on the coming mission by a plans-and-training officer over the public-address system. The situation was this:

The Japanese, in large numbers, were resisting strongly in the area around Ormoc, in the northwest portion of the island. Americans pressed against them from the north, south, and east. The 77th would come in by sea from the west.

Desmond and every man in the medical battalion knew there would be heavy fighting against strong resistance, and many casualties.

Desmond had mixed emotions about his new assignment. Though there were many new faces in both B Company and the 2d Platoon, some of the old-timers remained. It would be more dangerous, up there with the combat men, but Desmond was prepared for that type of work and believed he could be of greater service there. Not that his new designation as litter bearer was any picnic in combat. He was expected to go where the wounded lay and bring them back to the aid station for treatment. As he would be working out of the 1st Battalion aid station, which served Companies A, B, C, and D, he would still have some contact with his old unit.

The men hurry ashore from an LCI in the second stage of the end run at Ormoc. By interesting coincidence, Desmond Doss (arrow below) appears in the picture (U.S. Army photo).

Before dawn on the morning of December 8, cruisers and battleships of the United States Navy began a thunderous barrage against the coastline south of Ormoc. Desmond was in one of the first assault waves. Landing craft filled with soldiers shoved ahead, right into that inferno. Not until minutes before the first assault wave hit the beach did the big guns let up. Rockets continued to pass overhead, bursting behind the beaches. They made a frightening *whoosh, whoosh, whoosh* sound as they flashed overhead.

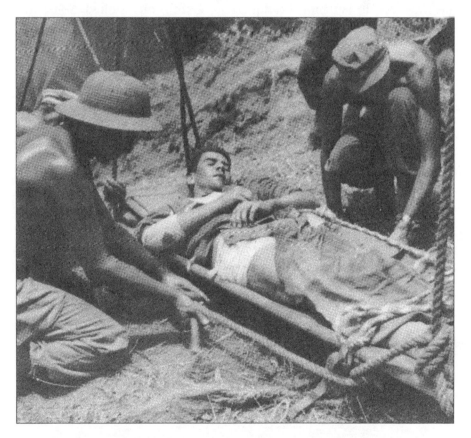

In the blistering Philippine sun, shirtless medics tie a wounded soldier's litter for transport across a ravine to an ambulance (U.S. Army photo).

This time the LCIs let down their landing ramps in shallow water, almost on the beach. The men poured off and ran lickety-split across the open beach toward the wall of jungle. Desmond's unit was lucky; they met virtually no opposition from the Japanese. It was later discovered that the Japanese were expecting reinforcements to be landed on that coast;

they thought the landing was made by their own forces. The 1st Battalion pressed on, crossing a road, slopping across a rice paddy, until it made contact with Japanese outposts at the village of Itil south of Ormoc. It took two days to secure Itil.

On the afternoon of the 8th, orders came down to B Company to advance across a stream and take the hill on the other side. D Company's machine guns furnished cover. When about half the company had crossed the stream, Captain Vernon received orders to pull the entire company all the way back to battalion headquarters. Confusion resulted. Some men still fought their way up the hill while others pulled back.

"What's it all about, anyway?" Lieutenant Gornto demanded.

American troops crossing a river to contact Japanese
near Ormoc, Leyte (U.S. Army photo).

"The Japs are counter-attacking on our right rear," Vernon said. "We've got to help beat them off."

Mortar shells began falling among the machine gunners on the hillside trying to protect the retreat. A shell fragment hit one of them in the head. His helmet went flying and blood gushed down into his eyes.

"Medic! Medic!" the cry went up.

Clarence Glenn heard the call. He and most of his company had now fallen back safely. He should stay with his own men. But again the call came. Glenn left his cover and dashed out into the open toward the wounded man. Ten yards before he reached his side, Glenn went down and lay motionless.

Now the machine gunners were ordered to fall back and they did so, leaving the two Americans lying there. Nobody knew whether they were alive or dead.

Word that Glenn was hit got back to Desmond Doss at the battalion aid station. Memories raced through his head—he, Glenn, and Dorris and their wives, together in the States. He thought of Glenn's wife and baby back home, and he knew he couldn't leave him there.

"I'm going after him," he said.

"There's another man out there too," somebody said. "The one Glenn went after."

"I'll go with you, Doss," Herb Schechter offered.

It was several hundred yards to the point where the two men had fallen. Only a few yards farther the jungle began. The Americans had pulled out. The Japanese were most assuredly approaching through the jungle beyond where the men lay.

Crouching, staying close to the ground, Desmond and Herb ran up the hillside toward the two wounded men. Both medics were veterans, and they handled themselves expertly, staying apart, now diving into a shell hole, now dashing forward again. Desmond reached the wounded man from Company D and threw himself down by his side just as Schechter reached Glenn.

Desmond examined the bloody face in front of him. The man had a large gash in his forehead. Blood had flowed into his eyes and dried. He was semiconscious and moaning. With a dressing and water from his canteen Desmond began gently wiping the wounded man's forehead and eyes. As the blood and grime came away, the fresh face of a mere youth appeared. The dried blood that covered his eyelids loosened, and the boy opened his eyes.

There on the battlefield, with bullets whizzing overhead and Japanese almost on top of them, the boy smiled. His face lighted up like a star shell.

"I can see, I can see," he whispered. "I thought I was blind."

For a fleeting moment Desmond shared his joy. He knew what was behind that smile. The boy had been hit, then he thought he was blind and left behind to die. Now life opened up for him again. That smile would remain in Desmond's memory as one of his greatest awards. It was for just this that the Army had trained him. But he could not delay too long.

"Can you move?" he asked. The soldier checked his limbs and nodded.

"Then start crawling back, and be careful. I've got to check this other man."

Several yards away Schechter lay beside Glenn.

"How is he?" Desmond called quietly.

"He's alive!" Schechter called back.

Bullets began whistling over their heads. The Japanese were firing in the direction of the two Americans' voices. Schechter jumped up and started running.

"Down, down!" Desmond cried. "Hit the ground. Play dead."

Schechter fell and lay motionless. Desmond was afraid his friend had been hit, and crawled toward him. But Herb was all right; he had followed Desmond's orders *too* realistically.

"No more talking," Desmond whispered. He crept on to Glenn. His friend was unconscious. Desmond did not take the time to examine him carefully. He had to get him out of there. Working clumsily and with difficulty while lying by his side, he eased Glenn's poncho off, spread it beside him, then rolled him over on it. Schechter crawled up and each grabbed a corner of the poncho.

The bullets still buzzed overhead, and the medics did not dare get even to their knees. Instead, lying on the ground, they hunched forward a few inches, then pulled the poncho up behind them. Fortunately they were going downhill. They had crawled only a few yards when they came to the body of a dead Japanese right in their path. They crawled over the body, dragged the poncho over it, and kept on going. It took well over half an hour to get down off the hillside and then to a thicket. There, for the first time, they could straighten up.

With the machete he carried for just that purpose, Desmond cut two poles and made a litter with them and the poncho. He and Herb eased Glenn's body onto the litter. Glenn's eyes opened. "It's me, Doss," Desmond whispered. He looked into Glenn's eyes for some sign of recognition. He clutched the injured man's hand and prayed.

"Oh, Lord, if it be Thy will, please spare this good man for those who love him. Amen."

Only a short prayer, but Desmond knew God would understand. He and Schechter picked up the litter and started back to the aid station. It was a clumsy burden, and they had a long way to go. The day was hot and muggy. They had to hold the poles not only up but out, in order to maintain pressure against the poncho and hold the litter together. They carried it for two or three hundred yards before taking a break.

Kneeling beside the litter, Desmond checked Glenn's pulse. The wounded man was unconscious but still breathing. When they got their breath they started forward again. There was still the danger of snipers, and they moved along quietly. They went up hill and down and splashed across two wide streams. They had to pause more often for rest now. The muscles in their backs, legs, and arms ached. Still they staggered on. Two stragglers, riflemen, appeared, and Desmond pressed them into service; now four men helped carry the litter. But it still weighed plenty.

Just ahead now lay the aid station. One more stop and they'd make it. They put Glenn down. Desmond knelt beside him. He felt for Glenn's pulse, but could feel none. In desperation he tried again. But Clarence Glenn was dead.

Grief-stricken, exhausted, dehydrated, Desmond remained on his knees motionless, almost in shock. He had lost his best friend. He had no desire to live. He did not even have the will to move. The other soldiers saw him, noticed his condition, and called Captain Tann. They removed his helmet and his medical kits, and got a handful of pills down his throat. Desmond didn't remember much after that. One of the pills, no doubt a sedative, enabled him to sleep the whole night through. Someone else obviously took his guard duty for him.

This combination of drugs and exhaustion helped ease the shock of his friend's death. In the morning he awakened physically refreshed, better able to put the loss of his friend out of his mind and carry on his duties.

The death of Glenn had one distinct aftereffect: From then on Desmond never wanted to look at the face of a man he was treating. He did not want to know his identity, lest it be another friend. He would treat all the wounded to the full extent of his knowledge and get them back to the aid station for treatment as quickly as he could, but the death of Glenn had hurt him so that he tried to protect himself against a recurrence.

One night's respite was all that Desmond could have. Heavy fighting continued, with frightening casualties. The Japanese took their toll, and tropical disease and the elements took theirs. Strong, sturdy feet that would carry an infantryman twenty-five miles with pack and rifle could not withstand constant moisture. Jungle rot, which reduced feet to red, painful stumps, prevailed throughout the division. At least, Desmond thought, he was not having to argue the merits of a case of jungle rot with Captain Vernon. The determined company commander could not understand such weakness.

On top of everything else, Desmond was not getting enough to eat. He lived on dog biscuits and coconuts. But even on Leyte, where coconut trees grew like pine trees in Virginia, there were not enough coconuts. The mature ones, those that had fallen from the trees, gave him diarrhea. In order to get the fresh ones, with pulpy meat he could eat with a spoon, he would have to climb the tall coconut palms.

The natives had cut notches in the tree trunks, but they were an incredible distance apart. A barefoot Filipino in a pair of shorts could climb with much less difficulty than a soldier in uniform and Army boots. But still Desmond tried. One day, moving up into position, the column stopped. Though Desmond was weak and exhausted, he climbed a tall tree and threw down several nuts to the men below. By the time he got down to the ground, with patches of skin missing from legs and arms, he found that the men had long since gone on, taking the coconuts with them.

Another time, in an almost identical situation, Desmond saw some coconut palms a hundred yards or so off the road behind a hedge. He started toward them, crossing a ditch. Suddenly the hedge seemed to erupt with machine gun fire—a Japanese ambush. There was Desmond, out in the middle of it looking for coconuts. He turned and ran for the ditch, diving into it headfirst. His own men returned the Japanese fire and wiped out the machine gunners. Not one American was hit. Investigation of the Japanese position showed why. Empty bottles were lying around; the Japanese had tanked up on sake, their rice wine, and were so drunk they couldn't have hit a battalion. It was the only time alcohol had ever been of benefit to Desmond Doss.

Crossing the Ormoc river was a major objective. The battalion had crossed and made some penetration into the terrain behind it, when it was decided that the penetration could not be held and the men should be pulled back across the river.

But one of the men far up the line had been hit. Desmond, carrying a litter, went after him. Across the river, he ran into a sergeant who seemed to be sight-seeing. The sergeant's job was to carry a heavy antitank gun, practically a cannon, on his back. It was the worst job in the company, and that morning the sergeant had announced he was through with it. He refused to carry the gun any further. Now he was due for a court-martial— yet here he was up in the farthest penetration.

"I'll help you, Doss," he volunteered. The two, now crawling, continued toward the Japanese, asking the whereabouts of the wounded man as they went. Orders were passed to withdraw, but six men volunteered to stay and cover them. Desmond and the sergeant continued on, and finally, practically within spitting distance of the Japanese, they heard moans and tracked them down. The man was conscious.

"Where are you hit?" Desmond asked.

"My foot," the man groaned.

"Your *foot*!" the sergeant exclaimed. "We risked our necks and you're hit in the *foot*?"

"It hurts," the man whimpered.

Desmond examined the wound. It was a bullet hole through the ankle and undoubtedly painful. But Desmond couldn't help feeling that if it had been his ankle he'd have crawled, dragging it after him, or even walked on it, rather than stay out there with the Japanese and wait for others to risk their lives.

He and the sergeant rolled the man onto the litter. They pushed it along a few inches at a time for some distance, then risked picking it up and running for short distances. They got the man back safely, wounded foot and all.

And the sergeant, who was brave enough to risk his life for a fellow soldier, was court-martialed and sent to prison in disgrace.

The Japanese were everywhere. They shot medics and litter bearers indiscriminately. But the wounded had to be cared for, and the medics had no choice. One day Desmond, Herb Schechter, and the other litter bearers were evacuating casualties across the Ormoc river. It was about 100 feet wide and only knee to hip deep, but no cover shielded them and they were exposed to sniper fire from up and down the river as they crossed over. Desmond was on the left front stirrup, Schechter on the right. They reached the bank and climbed it, trying to stay as small as possible.

At the top of the bank they were outlined against the sky for a swift second. Desmond heard a bullet whine by him. It hit Schechter. He pitched forward. His corner of the litter dropped and the wounded man fell off. Desmond pulled Schechter over the bank and ripped off his jacket. There was a hole in his back. He dusted it with sulfa and put a battle dressing on. He and the two other litter bearers hurried to the litter jeep with the man they had been carrying and came back with another litter for Schechter. He was still alive, and they carried him to the jeep. They were putting the litter on when a Japanese machine gun opened up. The driver jammed the accelerator down and the jeep leaped forward. Desmond shoved the litter forward as hard as he could, and it stayed on. Desmond ran after it. He caught hold of a bracket on the rear and held on, running, jumping, being dragged, and sailing through the air.

They reached the battalion aid station safely, but Schechter never regained consciousness. Another friend was gone. Again Doss could take no time to mourn.

The terrain was hilly in this part of Leyte. In the valleys, wherever the ground leveled off, rice had been planted and the ground flooded. Advancing across the paddies was particularly unpleasant, for they were anywhere from one to several inches deep in water, and especially dangerous because there was no cover.

In such a field a soldier was hit and cried out for a medic. The call passed back to the aid station, with the warning that the wounded man was in a dangerous and exposed position. Silence reigned for a long moment. No one wanted to go.

"Well, we can't leave him lying out there," Desmond said. "He could bleed to death while we're waiting for his position to be secured."

Desmond got the man's exact position from his fellow soldiers. "Be careful," they warned. "The sniper that got him is still out there." Desmond plotted his route carefully. He worked his way down the side of the hill, behind the retaining wall that surrounded the rice paddy. The wall petered out, but now he was at the paddy where the rice grew knee-high. It furnished some concealment and Desmond crawled out into it. On the hill behind him his buddies were firing across to the opposite hillside, keeping the enemy down, giving Desmond cover. Somewhere in this flooded field, he knew as he crawled through the water and mud, was a Japanese with a gun. Desmond could be in those gunsights at any moment. He refused even to think about it.

The soldier, someone he had never seen before, had been hit in the leg. The bone was broken, and he had lost a lot of blood. Lying by the man's side, Desmond bandaged the leg tightly. Then he began dragging the man back toward the retaining wall. It was slow going.

"Hey," he yelled. "Somebody come help me."

An infantryman jumped over the wall and zigzagged to his side. The wounded man put an arm around the shoulder of each, and they half carried, half dragged him to safety.

On top of the hill, one of Desmond's friends, a sergeant named Kelly, came running after him.

"Doss, I expected to see you killed any minute. We could all see it from up on the hill. You were crawling right toward that sniper! He had you in his sights for ten yards. The good Lord must have been with you that time."

Desmond felt a sinking sensation in his stomach, and the backs of his knees felt a little weak. He uttered a silent prayer of thankfulness. Other men kept coming up to him and commenting on his escape. Several of them had seen the whole thing.

Later, after he had taken the wounded man to the aid station, he thought about the miracle of the rice paddy. Perhaps the reason the Japanese did not fire was that he feared to give his position away. But more likely, Desmond felt, God directly intervened to keep him from pulling that trigger.

(Desmond was to tell this story frequently after the war. It became a part of Adventist lore, and was told all over the world, even in Japan. On one such occasion, a Japanese civilian came up after the services. "I must have been that sniper," he said. "I was in just such a situation and had a man in my sights as he crawled toward me. I tried to pull the trigger, but I could not.")

---

The 77th fought on—to Valencia, to Libungao, to Palompon.

The same miserable conditions continued. There wasn't a dry foot on the island. Desmond came into the aid station with a litter case to find a messenger from B Company waiting for him.

Captain Vernon had jungle rot, the messenger reported. After all the remarks he had made about the chancre mechanics and the pill rollers, he now needed one of them. And nobody in the medics was breaking his neck to take care of him.

"I'll fix his feet for him," one of the battalion surgeons said. "I'll fix 'em so he'll never walk on 'em again."

But Desmond was already slinging an aid kit over his shoulder. Although the visit entailed a hike through sniper-infested jungle, although

Captain Vernon's last words to him had been less than kind, Desmond never considered refusing to go. He was a medical soldier and a Christian. He'd take care of Vernon's feet.

At the company command post he found an unhappy captain. Vernon's feet were red with jungle rot, his face red with chagrin. Desmond knew what was going on in the captain's mind. The indestructible iron man lay in agony both mental and physical. He wanted to be out leading his men. After all the remarks he had made about the medics, he now had to eat crow and accept treatment.

"Hello, Doss."

"Hello, captain."

Neither said anything more. Desmond went to work efficiently and calmly. He treated the captain's feet as best he could, applying a special ointment and loose bandages. A better Man than he had once knelt at the feet of His disciples and washed them without making a fuss. Surely he, Desmond Doss, a medical soldier, could perform his duty with equal equanimity. When he finished, he advised Vernon to stay off his feet and keep them dry, two extremely unlikely courses of action, and turned to go. His former CO started to say something, but the words did not come. Desmond understood. It's hard for a man like Vernon, a company commander, to apologize and express gratitude to a private.

Shortly afterward the man who had replaced Doss as company aid man died suddenly with pneumonia. Doss went to Captain Tann and asked to be sent back to Company B.

"Doss, are you crazy?" the captain asked.

"No, sir. I'd just like to go back to my old buddies."

Captain Tann sighed and arranged for the transfer. When Desmond reported to Captain Vernon, the CO received him gruffly. He didn't say he was glad to see him. But, the formalities over, Vernon cleared his throat and said, "Doss, if there's anything in this company that isn't right, you tell me and I'll make it right. You understand?"

"Yes, sir." Desmond knew that in this way Vernon expressed both an apology and a welcome.

There could have been no worse time to rejoin B Company. The men fought exhaustion as much as the Japanese as they pushed through one village after another. The Japanese made forts out of every house and peppered the attacking Americans with small-arms fire. They had nothing to lose, for flame throwers would be brought up to ignite the buildings. None surrendered. They'd take as many men as they could before perishing in the flames.

In the all-out war in the Pacific, Desmond had little opportunity to show concern for the Japanese. He recognized them as fellow members of the kingdom of God, but with differences. Japanese-American members of the churches Desmond visited in Hawaii had told him that in Japan Christians were not given the opportunity to serve as medics. They either entered the army as combat soldiers or their throats were cut.

It was part of the military indoctrination to teach men to hate the enemy, and although Desmond never hated, the training did take some of the edge off his brotherly love. So many of his friends had been killed by Japanese, men like Herb Schechter, shot in the back while carrying a wounded man, and Clarence Glenn, that he could not help feeling some spirit of revenge. As for taking care of wounded Japanese, there were cases on record of these men lying on hand grenades and moaning for attention. When a medic rolled them over, the hand grenade went off, killing both. Japanese were told that they received some reward in their peculiar hereafter when they laid down their lives for the emperor, and taking an American along with them was even better.

The natives, both the Chamorros on Guam and the Filipinos, felt absolute hatred for the Japanese. They told of atrocities, of soldiers raping girls on the street in broad daylight, and killing anyone who protested. The few Japanese taken prisoner on Leyte had to be protected against the Filipinos. Desmond saw a group of natives, bolo knives in hand, running after a truckload of unarmed Japanese prisoners.

In spite of all this, when Desmond saw his first wounded Japanese he felt inclined to help them. They had been brought into the aid station and were lying there helpless. But an American soldier with a terrible stomach wound was lying with the same group of casualties. He kept crying out in his agony, pleading to be shot and put out of his misery. Desmond had done all he could for the American soldier and turned to the Japanese.

Two walking wounded men, still carrying their rifles, saw what he was about to do and raised their guns.

"If you touch one of those devils, Doss," one of the soldiers warned, "I swear to God I'll kill you."

And so Desmond Doss never treated any Japanese.

He treated everyone else who needed help. When the company dug in for the night, Captain Vernon posted guards around the company area and also had booby traps set. These were hand grenades arranged with a trigger wire so that anyone crawling into the company area would set them off.

One morning Desmond heard a grenade go off, followed by the screams of a child. He grabbed his aid kit and hurried in that direction.

"Wait a minute, Doss," one of the men cried. "We got to disconnect the booby traps."

When that was done, Desmond ran to the side of the victim, a little girl about five years old. She was bleeding from a dozen different places, including the nose; Desmond feared she had suffered a concussion. The company was in battalion relief and might be called upon at any minute, but Desmond remembered passing a small local dispensary with a nurse in attendance a few miles back. He wanted to take the girl there for attention. The company had two jeeps, but neither driver would take the child without Captain Vernon's permission. Doss ran to the captain.

"Both those jeeps are loaded and ready to go, Doss," Vernon said. "You can't have either one of them."

"And just let the little girl die?" Doss asked.

Vernon gave in. "Oh, all right," he said. "Unload one of them and take her on back."

The little girl's father came running up, and Doss put them both in the jeep. He went along too. He saw that she would be given good care at the dispensary, then hurried back. The company moved out only minutes after they returned.

One afternoon a Filipino came into the company area to seek medical aid for someone at home. He was passed along to "Doc," as the men called Desmond. The man's daughter had been wounded, Doss gathered, and he picked up his aid kit and went with him to see her. It was one of the worst wounds he had ever seen—open to the bone, infected, crawling with maggots, and exuding a foul-smelling discharge. Doss wiped it out with a sterile battle dressing, washed it with water, sprinkled it thoroughly with sulfa powder, then covered it with padding and a dressing.

The Japanese were putting up a stiff resistance there and the company remained in the area for a few days. When Desmond saw the girl again, the sore was healing nicely.

On another occasion he was dragged to a native hut to take care of a baby. "I'm not going to take care of no baby," he protested all the way. The Army had given him no course in pediatrics, but he did the best he could. The baby had a high fever, both nose and eyes running from crying. Desmond gave the baby a quarter of an aspirin-phenacetin-caffeine tablet to bring down the fever and left another quarter to be given in two hours. He told the family to boil water before giving it to the child. That was all he could do. Next day the young pediatrician returned to find the baby crawling around and laughing. Desmond got down on his knees and laughed with him. He'd saved his first baby.

An old man who lived near the bivouac area had been hit in the leg with a shell fragment. It had become infected, and gangrene had set in. Desmond treated it as best he could, but this was a case for the hospital. The old man refused to go, however, because he feared he would never see his family again. He was old and ignorant and afraid; as a matter of fact, Desmond had to communicate with him through an interpreter. Finally, however, Desmond prevailed upon him to go to the hospital for treatment and arranged transportation for him through a rear echelon outfit. Members of the family, who also called Desmond "Doc," were so grateful that they gave him bananas and their last egg. It was a little bitty egg laid by a scrawny, undernourished bantam chicken, and Desmond tactfully refused it.

On learning that Desmond was a Seventh-day Adventist, people in the village told him that other Adventists lived on the other side of the peninsula. He asked if it would be possible to visit them, and they eagerly agreed not only that it was possible, but that they would help him.

Desmond hurried back to the company area, packed up both of his aid kits, and came back. He and his equipment were packed into a flimsy canoe, made of canvas over bamboo with delicate outriggers. A fourteen-year-old boy served as his guide and paddler. Out to sea they glided, making surprisingly good time. They rounded the peninsula. Desmond, looking ashore, saw a dead Japanese soldier. It occurred to him for the first time that this side of the peninsula might not be cleared of Japanese.

He turned to the boy paddling and asked him if there were Japanese around. The boy shrugged. He did not know.

"What will we do if there are Japanese around and they start shooting at us?" Desmond asked.

"I will turn over the boat," his guide said, demonstrating with his hand, "and we will get under it."

"Oh," Desmond said. He did not bother to inform the boy that he could swim at best a half dozen strokes.

Fortunately no one fired upon them. After a great deal more paddling the boy turned in toward shore. As they came closer, Desmond saw women wading out into the water from the shore carrying earthenware jars. At a certain place they scooped up water into the jars, balanced them upright on their heads, and walked back to shore.

"What in the world are they doing?" Desmond asked.

"They are getting water," the boy explained. "It is a freshwater spring there."

Once ashore, Desmond was welcomed by the native people. They took him to a one-room schoolhouse where some twenty-five to thirty sick and wounded men lay on the floor. They were guerillas who had been fighting the Japanese. One native nurse, with limited knowledge and virtually non-existent supplies, attempted to take care of them. Desmond opened up his two aid kits on the spot. If he had brought them a million dollars in cash he could not have been more appreciated. He helped the nurse with some of the most serious cases and left all the contents of both bags.

"I know how our missionaries must feel," he remarked to Jim Dorris later. "It's a wonderful thing to be able to help people who are sick and in pain."

As the Leyte campaign continued, the bloodiest one yet, men fell all around Desmond, yet he was unharmed. He began to feel that he was receiving special protection from on high. Perhaps, he thought, physical exhaustion and emotional strain combined to make his fatigued brain more receptive to such a notion. Still, he could not put the thought out of his head that if he kept the Lord's commandments and did his work as best he could, he was keeping his share of a bargain and the Lord would keep His.

His regular reading of the Scriptures only enhanced this dream. He turned again and again to the ninety-first and ninety-third psalms, which, he believed, had a special message for him. The ninety-first in particular seemed to fit him exactly:

He that dwelleth in the secret place of the Most High shall abide under the shadow of the Almighty. I will say of the Lord, He is my refuge and my fortress: my God; in Him will I trust. Surely He shall deliver thee from the snare of the fowler, and from the noisome pestilence. He shall cover thee with His feathers, and under His wings shalt thou trust: His truth shall be thy shield and buckler.

Thou shalt not be afraid for the terror by night; nor for the arrow that flieth by day; nor for the pestilence that walketh in darkness; nor for the destruction that wasteth at noonday. A thousand shall fall at thy side, and ten thousand at thy right hand; but it shall not come nigh thee. Only with thine eyes shalt thou behold and see the reward of the wicked. Because thou hast made the Lord, which is my refuge, even the Most High, thy habitation; there shall no evil befall thee, neither shall any plague come nigh thy dwelling. For He shall give His angels charge over thee, to keep thee in all thy ways. They shall bear thee up in their hands, lest thou dash thy foot against a stone. Thou shalt tread upon the lion and adder: the young lion and the dragon shalt thou trample under feet.

Because he hath set his love upon Me, therefore will I deliver him: I will set him on high, because he hath known My name. He shall call upon Me, and I will answer him: I will be with him in trouble; I will deliver him, and honor him. With long life will I satisfy him, and show him My salvation.

How appropriate were these words! Desmond accepted them literally. He had never questioned one word in the Bible. He believed that men inspired by God, moved by God, had written each thought expressed. Therefore the Bible must be correct, all of it. The unfailing accuracy of the predictions of the prophets served as further proof.

And when the ninety-first psalm declared that "He shall give His angels charge over thee, to keep thee in all thy ways," Desmond Doss accepted this as a personal message.

But Desmond was still mortal, and he still had trials to face. As the company fought its way into the mountains, with hot days and cold nights, he began suffering alternate attacks of chills and fever. He shivered all night, and could not sleep. He had volunteered to help carry smoke grenades, but for the first time in his military career he found himself falling behind as the company moved forward.

"Come on, Doss," the men encouraged him. Even Lieutenant Gornto looked concerned, but he and the other men had their own problems to attend to. It was dangerous to fall behind, for the division moved too swiftly to clean out all the snipers. Desmond stumbled along, tired, cold, with a hacking cough. He never dreamed it was caused by anything but the cold nights.

Strange things happened to many men during this period of continuous combat. During his entire period of service with the 307th, Desmond had kept running into that one soldier who symbolized all the ugliness, the evil, which was to be found in the Army as in any group of men chosen from all walks of life. He was the man named Karger,[4] the older, cynical

---

4   A pseudonym.

product of the big-city slums who had first snarled at him that lonely night back in Fort Jackson when the shoes had come sailing over the bunks. It was the same man who had accused him of goldbricking at the rifle range, and told him, "Doss, if we ever get in combat there's one man who's not coming back alive. That's you." This was a man who seemed to care about nothing but himself and his own creature comforts. If there was any whiskey or sake, the Japanese wine, or native brew to be found, this man would find it.

During the worst part of the Leyte campaign, Desmond saw this veteran troublemaker coming toward him. He prepared himself for the inevitable stream of curses. Instead the soldier planted his feet, looked at Desmond through bloodshot eyes, and asked, bluntly, directly, "Doss, pray for me." For a moment Desmond couldn't speak; then he recovered his tongue.

"Why come to me? I'm no chaplain."

"I already went to the chaplain, and all he could offer me was a drink. The chaplain's no better than I am. But you believe your religion. My time's runnin' out. Pray for me, Doss."

"I will," the medic promised, "but you've got to pray for yourself."

"I dunno how. But when I get back to the States I'm gonna start goin' to church."

Desmond reached out and clutched his arm. "You can't wait that long! We don't have that kind of insurance. You've got to begin now."

The man was near tears. "Doss, you're the only man in this outfit who has any religion. Help me."

"There are lots of men with religion here. Listen. The Lord can help you to live for what you know to be right. He will help you just as He has been helping me. You've got to make up your mind to prepare to meet your Maker in case your time should come."

"I'll try, I'll try," the soldier whispered. "Thank you." He turned and trudged off toward his own outfit. Desmond never saw him again.

All campaigns must come to a close. The 307th's active participation in the Leyte campaign ended with the capture of the vital Libungao road junction. This completed the Ormoc campaign with a decisive victory which led to the liberation of the Philippines. For continuing bravery during this important campaign Desmond was recommended for the Bronze Star.

The 77th Division moved into a rest area. While the rest of the men ate, slept, made plans with the local people, and swam in the blue Pacific, Desmond Doss stayed in the pup tent he shared with James Dorris and slept, slept, slept. Frequently he couldn't even go to the chow line. Dorris would bring him back something to eat. Gradually he felt himself regaining his strength. After two lazy weeks he was ready to go again.

And this was fortunate, for the most demanding ordeal of all was yet to come.

# CHAPTER 5

## ONE BUSY SABBATH

"**H**ey, Doss," one of the new replacements called, "have you heard the latest? Because we've been through two rough campaigns they're gonna make us a reserve of reserves in this next one. That's pretty good, huh?"

Desmond sighed. So many replacements—it was practically a new outfit. He didn't even know this young soldier's name. "Yeah, sounds pretty good," he replied. No point in telling him what the old-timers knew. "Reserve of reserves" sounded good all right, but what it really meant was that the 77th would be held out until the situation was desperate, then thrown into the toughest, bloodiest fighting of all. That's the way it always worked. They had barely finished up the Leyte campaign and here they were getting ready to fight again.

Desmond couldn't help feeling some bitterness. Months before they'd been promised a rest on New Caledonia; well, they hadn't even *seen* New Caledonia. He was now supposed to have a Bronze Star, but he hadn't seen that either. Even if he had it, he could just see himself pinning it on his dirty fatigues.

Captain Tann had taken it on himself to get his men promotions, and now Desmond was a private first class. After almost three years in the Army, he was one grade above the bottom, with a base pay increase from $50 a month to $54. Big deal.

In the spring of 1945, it was obvious to any American in the South Pacific that from here on any operation would be a major, hard-fought struggle. As the Americans came closer to the Japanese homeland, the Japanese resisted fanatically. Wherever the next battle would be, Desmond knew, it would be the fiercest challenge to the division and to himself.

With the rest of the 1st Battalion, Company B left the bivouac area on Leyte and boarded the U.S.S. *Mauntrail.* This was the company's fourth transport. Looking around him, Desmond saw some of the old familiar faces on board—Captain Vernon and Lieutenant Gornto, of course, and Lieutenant Phillips and Lieutenant Onless C. Brister, who'd also seen a lot of action. There were two other Virginians in the company, William S. Carnes and Lewis R. Brooks, whom he knew well, and, of course, his fellow medic Jim Dorris. Some of the noncoms, like Sergeant Kunze, had been given battlefield commissions and transferred as officers to other companies. Privates and Pfc's had been promoted. Joseph R. Potts, Charles C. Edgette, and Clarence O'Connell were sergeants now, on their way up. Staff Sergeant John Maholic, always one of the best-liked men in the company, had

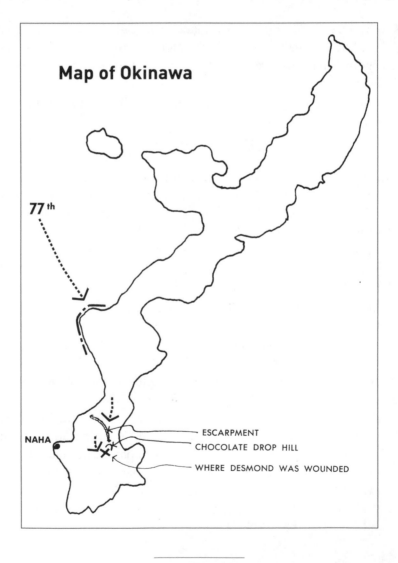

proved himself again and again in combat, and was one of the most respected men in the outfit and the most popular.

But the missing faces outnumbered those present. Glenn and Schechter and the others—Desmond quickly pulled his mind away. Such thoughts were dangerous. Northward steamed the convoy, northward until it seemed that Japan itself was just over the horizon. Late in the day of March 23, a big island appeared. It was Okinawa, in the Ryukyus, little more than 500 miles from the southernmost island of Japan. It was common knowledge that the island bristled with weapons and was defended by large numbers of the enemy's finest troops.

Other units of the 77th participated in comparatively minor engagements on the smaller islands surrounding Okinawa. Company B didn't leave the ship, but it was in a constant war of its own. For it was during this period that the Japanese introduced the Kamikazes, or suicide planes. The *Mauntrail* was under constant attack. During one five-minute period the ship shot down three Japanese planes. The *Mauntrail* stayed off the coast of Okinawa for almost a month with its reserve of reserves, fighting off swarms of Kamikazes. Almost with relief the men of the 1st Battalion, 307th Regiment, learned that they would be getting off this ship and going into combat.

"It must be pretty rough or they wouldn't be calling us this soon," one of the men observed.

"It's always rough," Desmond answered. "But with God's help we'll do all right."

Ashore, the men quickly heard many of the gory details of that strange and tragic campaign. The Japanese had convinced the natives that the Americans would torture and slaughter them. Horrified young Americans saw native mothers cut their children's throats, then their own, as the soldiers approached. In a hysterical madness that caught all the civilians on the island, they slaughtered themselves and each other.

The Okinawans buried their dead in large caves marked by strange, ornate entrances. Moving into the front lines, Company B stopped for the night just short of the combat zone. It was a desolate, fought-over area with shot-up tanks and destroyed shacks. As the men dug in for the night, Desmond noticed one of the odd-looking tombs within the company perimeter and entered it. It was dark and damp and permeated with a heavy, sweetish odor.

Several large earthen urns stood in the back of the cavern; Desmond peered into one. In the dim light he saw a skeleton. Desmond figured that this would be the last place a Japanese would enter. He bedded down in the tomb for the night. Darkness had hardly settled, however, before he realized he had made a whopping big mistake. He was alone and unarmed. If the Japanese came in, he was helpless. What was worse, he couldn't leave. If he came crawling out of that tomb at night he'd be shot to pieces by his own men. It was a long night, and, as Desmond ruefully admitted to his buddies next morning, he did more praying than sleeping.

Before the soldiers advanced to their positions next morning, Captain Vernon pointed out the terrain to the company. The bivouac area was on a small ridge, looking to the south. The American forces had cut the island in two and were working southward. The major Japanese fortifications and forces occupied the rugged limestone hills of the southern part of the island.

Across the littered valley rose another brown rocky ridge, known as the Maeda Escarpment. Its slopes rose sharply from the valley, covered with huge boulders. At the top of the slope stood a sheer rock cliff, from 30 to 50 feet high. Maeda Escarpment commanded the entire width of the island. From it the Japanese could see the activities of the advancing forces from sea to sea and for many miles back. It had to be taken.

"On top of that hill and behind it," Captain Vernon told the men, "the enemy has built a complex of pillboxes, fortifications, and emplacements. Two divisions have been cut to pieces trying to take that hill. Now it's up to us. We will move up and take our position at the bottom of the cliff. From there we will study the situation and make our plans."

The men looked around at each other. Company B had undertaken some dangerous missions, but nothing like this. Several of the men looked at Desmond. He tried to appear calm and reassuring. He knew his importance to their morale. A good medic could mean the difference between life and death, and Desmond Doss had proved himself to be a good medic, over and over.

In the early morning, under cover of darkness, the company moved into its new position at the base of the cliff. There were big rocks piled together, making crevices, covering caves. Under the protection of the cliff the company area seemed fairly safe.

That afternoon Lieutenant Gornto and Sergeant Potts explored the cliff, and determined where it could be scaled. They cautiously climbed it and, keeping low, peered out across the hill. They identified several concrete-and-steel pillboxes and emplacements. They sent back to battalion headquarters for rope, a large supply of demolition equipment, and flamethrowers. Next day they'd attack the escarpment.

At daybreak Potts and Edgette had their squads ready. Desmond was with them. He knew they wanted him along. He was scared, but he was also curious. He had a captured pair of Japanese binoculars, and he hung them around his neck. If the view from the escarpment was so great, he wanted to see it!

Maeda Escarpment as seen from the American side. Line X-X indicates where the assault was made; line Y-Y, Company B area, protected by cliff.

One by one, laboriously, they scaled the cliff. At the top, keeping prone, creeping on their bellies, they collected loose rocks—there were hundreds of them—pushed them forward, and built a kind of rock wall a few feet back from the edge of the cliff for protection. They secured one end of the rope to a boulder and dropped the other end over the cliff, for reinforcements. Another squad climbed up this way. It was easier going. By keeping low, presenting little target, the small force managed to avoid drawing enemy small-arms fire. There was no work for Desmond, and he squirmed around to face northward. The military importance of the escarpment immediately became apparent. He could see every phase of American military activity to the rear. Out to sea he saw transports at anchor and landing craft bringing supplies. A geyser of seawater went up near one as a Japanese shell exploded. They were sitting ducks.

The escarpment on Okinawa at the point where Company B made its first assault, and where Doss lowered the wounded. This picture, taken only two days after the first assault (the one Doss started off with a prayer) led by Gornto, shows the cargo net and the rope later used to lower the wounded. Desmond himself is standing at the top of the cliff. At upper right, just out of the picture, is the tree around which he took a loop of the rope. The carrying cases below are placed on top of a protective wall made of rocks piled by hand. Above the cases are stalactite-like formations like the ones where Doss spent the night with a sleepy soldier.

*Whump!* The sound of an explosion came from the other side of the low rock wall. Another, and another, this time from behind them at the base of the cliff. Desmond had heard that sound before.

"Mortars!" he shouted. "Knee mortars!"

Knee mortars could be fired at such an angle of elevation that they could drop almost straight down. The little rock wall furnished no protection against a mortar attack. The Japanese were zeroing in; it was only a matter of minutes.

"Pull back," the word was passed. "Get back down the cliff."

Captain Vernon sent word of the withdrawal back to Battalion, and received orders to continue the attack the next day. Company A would also attack, higher on the escarpment, to the left. Three large cargo nets, the kind thrown over the side of the ship for debarkation purposes, were sent out from Battalion. Pieces of timber were used to thread the three together into one large net.

As dawn approached, Lieutenant Gornto called Doss to him. "You were pretty good with knots back in mountain training," Gornto recalled. "How about helping us secure these nets to the top of the cliff?"

"Yes, sir," Doss said. He and a couple of other men, lines secured to their belts, climbed the cliff. Keeping low, Desmond secured the end of his rope to a large boulder. Then they pulled up the net and made it fast. The entire platoon could now swarm the cliff almost in a body. Preparations complete, Desmond and the other men climbed back down the nets.

Gornto would lead the assault. The major objective was a huge pillbox several yards back from the edge of the cliff. It was from this fortified vantage point that the Japanese were able to call down that dangerous mortar fire. Gornto assembled a squad of the toughest veterans, beginning with the three sergeants, Potts, Edgette, and O'Connell. Desmond volunteered.

"This is going to be a dangerous mission, Doss," Gornto told him. "You don't have to go."

"I feel I should, lieutenant," Desmond said. "I may be needed. But, lieutenant, I'd like to ask a favor before we go."

"OK, Doss, what is it?" Gornto said.

"Sir, I believe that prayer is the biggest lifesaver there is. I believe that every man should have a word of prayer before he puts his foot on the rope ladder to go up that cliff."

What Desmond meant was that each man should have the opportunity to say a silent prayer himself. Gornto, however, called the group of men together and told them that Doss was going to lead them in prayer.

Desmond had not thought about making a formal prayer, but he did not let his lack of preparation delay him. He stepped forward and said the first words that came into his heart.

The top of the escarpment, viewed along its length. C and D are blown up Japanese positions. Arrow points to Japanese fortified position blown by Lieutenant Phillips. It is concealed by a hill. X marks trees where a Japanese knee mortar was located. Note the shell holes in the foreground.

"Our heavenly Father," Desmond prayed, "please give our lieutenant wisdom and understanding so that he can give us the right orders, because our lives will be in his charge. Please give each and every one of us the wisdom and understanding concerning how to take all the safety precautions necessary in order that, if it be Thy will, oh, Lord, we may all come back alive. And further we ask that if there be any here who are not prepared to meet their Maker, they prepare themselves now through prayer before they climb the cliff. We ask all this in Jesus' name."

For another moment the war on the escarpment stood still as the men remained motionless. Desmond was positive that all were praying, even those who had never prayed before. Then, confident, almost carefree, they turned to the cargo net at the bottom of the cliff, signaling to Company A to the west that they were beginning the assault. The members of the suicide squad, with their medic at their heels, climbed the cliff and without hesitation moved on across the top of the hill toward the enemy pillbox.

Two tanks, a thousand yards back, poured in a coordinated fire on the pillbox. It was ineffective. Now Gornto beckoned Pfc Norman Black to come up with his bazooka. Black fired several times. The explosions uncovered an aperture in the side of the concrete dome. Under cover of two automatic riflemen from the flanks, one of the men ran forward and threw a satchel charge of explosives into the pillbox. Heavy logs which had obviously formed a part of the fortification flew up like matchsticks. A soldier rushed to it with a flamethrower and directed its full force into the gaping hole.

No more resistance came from it, and the entire assault squad moved forward. They saw only a large hole; the sides had caved in, covering whatever openings had been there before.

View along the escarpment with the American position at right and the sea in the distance. A is where Colonel Maddox was fatally wounded; B, the line of the cliff top. The arrow points to a handmade rock wall along the top of the cliff. C is the first pillbox blown by Lt. Gornto. D is a pinnacle that rises behind the Company B area at base of cliff.

Covered by a light machine gun mounted on the pillbox, Gornto's squad moved out over the hilltop. They blew up several other pillboxes in the immediate area. Now the Japanese behind the edge of the hill began throwing hand grenades on the advancing Americans. The forward men in the squad threw grenades back. A furious battle ensued.

Desmond was making himself small in a hole behind the rock wall. The forward men ran out of grenades and cried for more to be passed up. A box of grenades suddenly appeared at the top of the cliff.

"Pass 'em on," the soldier who had carried them up said. Desmond looked over the wall. The next man was several feet away. If he came back, crawled over the little wall, picked up the grenades and returned, he'd be an easy target coming and going. It would be his life, and the men forward would not have their grenades. It would be their lives too.

Desmond picked up the grenades and passed them over the wall. It was the first and only time he touched a lethal weapon.

In the meantime Company A had failed to take its assigned position. The first five men to reach the top of the cliff had been killed instantly.

But the Company B assault squad had secured a large area on the top of the escarpment. Gornto and Desmond looked around for any wounded who might need attention, and also for the dead. But there were none. In all this furious action the squad from Company B had had just one injury. Sergeant O'Connell's hand had been hit by a piece of flying rock!

This was incredible—to everyone except Desmond. Had he not prayed?

Captain Vernon sent the third platoon up on the escarpment to relieve the assault squad. Desmond stayed on top. He sensed that he would be needed, and he was. The end had come to that miraculous period in which a large group of men operated under a hail of Japanese bullets and hand grenades with no serious wound. It was as though Desmond's prayer had specifically covered one group of men for one period of time. Now that group had retired to safety, and the time was over. The cry "Medic" went up again and again, and Desmond crawled all over the hilltop ministering to the wounded. Then he would help them to the edge of the cliff and down the cargo net.

Night came, but it brought no peace, no quiet. Japanese artillery and mortar fire increased. After midnight a large group of Japanese rushed the men on the escarpment, throwing grenades, then joining in hand-to-hand combat. The Americans were forced down off the escarpment. And in the meantime, Japanese suddenly began appearing beneath the cliff. They oozed out of holes and crevices. For the first time the company realized that the honeycombing of the hill extended out into their own area. The enemy was underneath them!

When dawn broke after a wild night, Desmond Doss had gone to the aid of eighteen men, including Potts and Edgette. Lieutenant Brister was in shock. Four of the eighteen men were dead. One of them was a company aid man who had just come in as a replacement. During the night he had reached out of his hole for his canteen and was shot through the head.

But as soon as dawn broke, Captain Vernon had his men moving forward again to recapture what they had lost during the night. Again Desmond was with them. One episode followed another. A lieutenant was leading three men in a running attack on an emplacement. The lieutenant drew back his hand to throw a grenade. A bullet hit him, delayed the throw. The grenade went off, taking his hand with it, and wounding the other three men. It all happened right in front of Doss. In a swift second, he had four men to take care of there on the bullet-swept hilltop.

He fell to his knees among them. Men behind him were throwing grenades over his head into the Japanese lines. They saw Desmond, and the word passed up and down the line to be careful. The grenades stopped coming. The Japanese began peering over the hillside to see what caused the cessation.

"Don't stop now!" Desmond shouted back to his men. "Keep 'em coming!"

The fellows started throwing grenades over his head again and to either side, keeping the Japanese down so he could finish the job. He had to stanch the flow of blood from the lieutenant's stump as well as from other wounds, and put dressings on the wounds of the three other men. Two of them could crawl, and Desmond sent them back on their own. He grabbed the lieutenant by the collar and hunched him, a few inches at a time, back toward the edge of the cliff. An infantryman ran up and helped the fourth soldier get back to his lines.

A little later Desmond was crouched on the hillside watching a fellow soldier attack the mouth of a Japanese-held cave. The man fired several shots into the cave, then took his satchel charge and started to heave it in. Just as it left his hand a bullet struck him. As Desmond watched, he saw the man's teeth fly out.

"Cover me!" Desmond shouted to a pair of infantry men inching their way forward behind him. As they fired into the cave, Desmond ran to the wounded man, ripped open his shirt, located a hole in his chest through which the blood was pouring, and slapped a heavy dressing on it. The soldier was unconscious, but Desmond raised him up and got his arm over his shoulder. Clutching the wounded man's arm with one hand, holding onto his waist with the other, Desmond ran toward his own lines, dragging the wounded man with him. They reached the edge of the cliff. But it had been a needless mission. The soldier was dead.

"Medic, medic!" came the shout. Desmond had no time to mourn. A shell had fallen in a machine gun emplacement far up the hill to the left. Desmond, stooped low, zigzagging, ran to the spot. Little was left of one of the men, just a disembodied hand still clutching the machine gun. The shell had blown the lower leg off the other man. His thigh was already swelling. Desmond bound it tightly, then began dragging the machine gunner toward the nearest point at the top of the cliff. A deep ravine cut through his path. A wooden ladder leaned against the side of the ravine. Desmond pulled it up and extended it across to the other bank of the ravine; it just reached.

A rifleman was watching from a shell hole. "Help me!" Desmond said in a voice that was half plea, half command. The soldier came to his aid. Desmond backed out on the ladder, dragging the wounded man's head and shoulders. The soldier followed, helping as best he could. The ladder was old and rickety. It had been spliced in two places. It bent and creaked, but Desmond kept going, and his helper followed. The ladder held, and they got the man to safety.

Day followed day, and still the fighting continued. The nights were as bad. Up on the escarpment the Japanese kept up a constant grenade barrage and continued to infiltrate. Below, at the base of the cliff, it was even more dangerous. Men would find a crevice in the rocks, crawl into it, barricade the front, and sink into a coma of exhaustion. From behind them Japanese would silently sneak out of a hole in the rear of the crevice and slit the Americans' throats while they slept.

But an even greater danger was the endless barrage of mortar shells. In some places along the cliff the base was eroded away, and the overhang furnished excellent protection. In front of one of these places rocks had been piled up to furnish additional defense.

One night Desmond shared this cavern-like refuge with a rifleman in the 2d Platoon. He noticed a large hole in the back of the crevice, but it seemed to go nowhere. Nevertheless, they decided it would be wise for one to stay awake while the other slept, two hours on and two off. Desmond took guard first, sitting back near the edge of the hole. After a few minutes he heard a rustling noise, then someone whispering. The sounds

This Japanese ladder was spliced together to bridge a ravine so that a wounded man could be carried to safety. The black space behind it is one of the scores of holes and caves that dot this part of Okinawa.

came from the hole—and the whispering was in Japanese! He awakened the soldier with whom he shared the hole and whispered to him to listen.

"Uh huh," the soldier mumbled, and resumed snoring. Desmond lay awake, hardly daring to breathe himself, listening to the mysterious sounds coming from the unseen enemy just a few feet away.

When it was time for the rifleman to take his turn on watch, Desmond woke him again. Within five minutes the fellow was snoring. And again the ominous rustlings came from beneath.

All night Desmond tried to get his partner to pull his turn at guard. He would promise to do so, but would not stay awake two minutes. Desmond tried to get him to change places with him. At least then, if the Japanese came out of the hole, they'd find the sleeping guard first. But though almost comatose, the soldier was too smart to change positions.

The sleeping soldier had two hand grenades. Just one, dropped down that hole, would put an end to the danger, and Desmond could go to sleep himself. That night was the closest Desmond ever came to taking life, for he considered dropping those grenades. But he put the idea out of his mind. Though it could well become a matter of life or death for himself, Desmond would not break the sixth commandment.

And so he stayed awake the entire night. During that night he came to one firm conclusion: If he lived through it, God willing, he'd never spend another night either in that hole or with that soldier.

The next night he kept both those resolutions, holing up with Gornto in a protected place serving as the platoon command post. Just before dawn Desmond heard the familiar cry, "Medic, medic!" Intuition told him what had happened.

"You don't have to go, Doss," Lieutenant Gornto said, but Desmond felt he had no choice.

"Pass the word along that I'm coming, so they won't shoot me," he said. Feeling his way in the dark, whispering reassuringly in the hill-country accent no Japanese could mimic, to calm itchy trigger fingers, he proceeded to the cave where he had spent the previous wakeful night.

Inside was one soldier. Another lay several feet away. Both were torn and bleeding, victims of grenades. Probably the grenades had come from the hole where he had heard the Japanese whispering the night before. Desmond used up all his large battle dressings on the wounded men and sent them back to the aid station at daybreak. But he did not believe they could survive.

The escarpment continued to hold up the entire American advance. Higher commands from division headquarters to the Pentagon were concerned about the Japanese resistance on that honeycombed hill. Press dispatches told the entire nation about the battle raging there. Of particular interest was the account of the first day's battle in which no one had been seriously injured, no one killed. Such operations just don't happen. A Signal Corps photographer came to the company CP two or three days after Gornto had led the assault squad up the cliff.

"I understand you had a fantastic operation here," the photographer said, "blowing a dozen pillboxes and not having one man killed."

"That's right." Captain Vernon explained the situation. The Signal Corps photographer looked at the cargo nets.

"We'll send somebody up with you so you can get pictures from on top," Captain Vernon volunteered.

"Oh, no," the photographer said quickly. "I can take the pictures from down here."

It was Desmond Doss and Jim Dorris who climbed up the cargo net and stood at the top of the cliff, for the photographer's benefit.

"C'mon up," Desmond called. He and Dorris were fairly well concealed by the natural slope and the rock wall that had been built the first day.

But the photographer did not appreciate the invitation. "I haven't lost anything up there," he explained.

Fighting on the fire-swept escarpment by day, prey of the enemy slipping out of caves by night, even seasoned veterans began to show fear. All around him Desmond saw the drawn faces, the staring eyes, the twitching hands of extreme mental strain. One of the top noncoms of the company sought out Desmond and told him, "I can't go on any longer. My luck's run out. You can say I'm sick. You got to send me back."

Doss shook his head. He understood the man's fears, but he could not approve. "There's nothing the matter with you," he said. "Stop talking like that. Pull yourself together and you'll be all right."

He later heard that the sergeant was going around offering to pay other soldiers to shoot him in the leg or arm.

On the other hand, a corporal, one of the original members of the company and a man who had given his best from the first day he had joined the outfit, came down with some ailment which resulted in a high fever and swollen glands. His entire neck was swollen, red and painful to the touch. He couldn't turn his head; he had to move his entire body to look to the side. With such pain, and under such a handicap, he could not possibly take care of himself on the escarpment. Desmond sent him back to the battalion aid station. A few hours later, here came the corporal back again. The medical officer at the aid station had told him to go back to duty and "take it easy."

"How can you take it easy up here?" Desmond demanded. He was actually angry. "You go back to battalion aid station, and you tell them that I said you are in no fit condition to be up here. If the doctor wants to see me about it, I'll come back and talk to him. But don't you come back up here. You understand?"

The little corporal with the swollen neck started the long trip back to the battalion aid station again. Desmond watched him go. "That's a good man with not one cowardly drop of blood in his entire body," he fumed for the benefit of anyone who would listen. "I won't let them send him back up here to get killed."

The dead lay everywhere. On top of the escarpment both Americans and Japanese lay where they had fallen. Down below, the American dead were removed, but nobody took the time to pick up the enemy bodies. A Japanese officer who had infiltrated the company area and killed two of Desmond's buddies before being killed himself lay sprawled over a rock. His dead hand still clutched his saber. That saber would have brought $100 from the souvenir hunters in the rear echelons or the Navy, but none of the men up front even looked at it.

But all this death had to have some effect. Desmond worried more about the buddies he was losing every day than about himself. One day, moving like a sleepwalker, he went through the GI ritual of pouring some gasoline into a tin can, then throwing in a match to make a quick fire to heat his food. He sat on his heels and watched the flame. He felt moisture on his cheeks and brushed it away with his knuckles. For the first time he realized that he was crying. Then he looked at the fire that he had just built.

"Why am I doing this?" he asked himself. "I'm not hungry!"

He realized that he had to pull himself together, stop thinking about his good friends who had been killed—too many of them—and replace his trust in the Lord.

The fighting for the escarpment continued day after bloody day, night after fearful night. Though the enemy had been pretty well cleared off the top of the hill, an area about as wide as a football field, the slope on the other side was dotted with pillboxes leading to the maze of tunnels beneath. By day the Americans occupied the top of the hill, attempting to push forward. By night the Japanese crept out of their holes and slithered soundlessly over the terrain.

A key Japanese emplacement, really just a fortified gaping entrance to the tunnels beneath, was spotted just over the lip of the far slope of the escarpment. The Americans tried to hit it with mortars and artillery, but it was protected by the slope of the hill. Repeated efforts were made to knock it out. Sergeant John Maholic, the popular noncom from the heavy weapons platoon, got close enough to throw a grenade in. The Japanese threw it right back out again. Under cover of friendly fire two engineers ran forward and dumped in a satchel charge. The Japanese pulled the fuses before it could explode.

Someone at headquarters got the brilliant idea of fashioning a trough out of tin to run all across the hill. Gasoline poured into the trough at the American side would flow across into the Japanese hole. Then a grenade thrown in would ignite it. But laying the trough was a clumsy operation, and there wasn't enough elevation for the gas to flow. Japanese continued to emerge from the hole.

Army medics strain to carry litter over difficult Okinawa
terrain en route to an aid station (U.S. Army photo).

"I'm going to blast that hole if it kills me," Sergeant Maholic said. He led a squad of volunteers across the top of the escarpment to the lip of the hill. As his men covered him, he jumped up and ran toward the hole, a grenade in each hand.

Bullets thudded into the sergeant's body as he ran. He staggered, then fell. His momentum carried him almost to the edge of the hole. He lay there, still. The grenades rolled on and exploded harmlessly.

"Maholic's hit!" the word got back to Doss. He was helping a wounded man on top of the escarpment. Though it was almost certain that Maholic was dead and Desmond was numb with exhaustion, he went forward without hesitation. He knew the respect the men had for Maholic. A man from his squad accompanied Doss, and together they crawled almost to the very lip of the hole. They grabbed Maholic's feet and dragged his body back up the hill and to the cover of a shell hole. There Desmond examined him. John Maholic was dead. From the nature of his wounds, he had probably died instantly.

As an ambulance jeep evacuates three wounded men to a rear area field hospital on Okinawa, one of them is given blood plasma by a 102d Med. Bn. corpsman (U.S. Army photo).

Word swept through the company, and was taken back to the battalion headquarters by the wounded: Desmond Doss, who had risked his life so many times to save the wounded, had done it again for a dead man.

That afternoon Desmond had to go back to the battalion aid station to pick up supplies. Captain Tann greeted him with, of all things, an admonition.

"What's this I hear about you risking your neck to save a dead man?" he railed. "You'll only succeed in getting yourself killed that way, and dead medics are no good to anybody. If I ever hear of you doing anything like that again, I'll pull you back."

But even as he talked his voice softened. Desmond Doss looked as if he had been fighting a war all by himself. His face was drawn. He was edgy and irritable. His hands trembled. His uniform was brown with the blood of men he had treated and dragged to safety, and with his own blood, for a flying rock had cut a nasty gash.

The day was ending. "You're going to spend the night here, Doss," Captain Tann told him.

"Oh, no, captain, I'd better get back to the company," Desmond said.

"You'll stay here and that's an order," Tann said. "We're going to feed you and see to it that you get some sleep. I don't even want you to pull any guard duty."

After chow the captain directed Desmond to a quiet cave. An underground stream bubbled with a soothing sound. After his nightly prayers Desmond opened up a litter and stretched out on it. Before he could really appreciate the security, the quiet, and the soft murmur of the brook, he was sound asleep.

In the morning, refreshed after his first full night's sleep since going up to the escarpment, Desmond realized how close he had been to complete exhaustion, both physical and mental.

Before he left the aid station, litter bearers brought in a lieutenant from another company. He was a young officer, and he was worried that all of his men were going to be killed in a forthcoming attack.

"I've got to get to them; I've got to get to them!" he kept crying. "Don't you understand? Help me get to my men!" His eyes were bloodshot, his nose running, his face contorted. He kept trying to get off the litter, but he was in such an hysterical state that he could barely move his arms. When Desmond last saw him, he was lying there weeping helplessly.

"That almost happened to me," Desmond thought, and resolved again, with the help of God, to keep his nerves under control.

It was another rough day on the escarpment. Dorris was wounded; now Desmond was the only medic for the entire company. He holed up that night with Gornto and five of his riflemen. Surely this would be a large enough force both to enable him to get some rest between standing guard duty and to guarantee protection against enemy soldiers infiltrating the company area. They had found an indentation in the side of the cliff against which a flat rock leaned, and had piled up fired mortar shells filled with rocks to close in one side. A rock parapet stood on the other side.

Desmond pulled guard first. Nearby a mortar squad was firing, keeping the Japanese from moving around on top of the escarpment. After several *whumps,* he heard a different sound, the explosion of a grenade. Desmond saw, standing on the parapet outside, outlined against the sky, a Japanese soldier.

"Lieutenant!" he whispered, and pointed the soldier out to Gornto.

"We'll get him," Gornto said. But firing from the darkness through the narrow aperture was difficult. The bullets missed. But the Japanese saw the flashes. He began trying to throw grenades through the opening. It was just a question of time before he'd get one in and wipe out all seven of them. The men inside were trapped. Desmond realized that this time death was inevitable. He started to pray for Gornto and the other men as well as for himself.

And the Lord heard his prayer. Gornto had left his pack outside the cave. In it were two white phosphorus grenades. The next grenade flung by the Japanese landed on that pack. Somehow, instead of exploding, the phosphorus grenades merely burned. A great cloud of white smoke resulted. The wind was just right, and blew it over the enemy soldier. He couldn't take it.

"Let's get out of here!" Gornto hollered. One after the other they squeezed through the narrow aperture. Desmond, handicapped by his aid kits, had to let the others go first. The billowing clouds of smoke had almost dissipated by the time he got out of the cavern.

Running hard in the darkness, he was on Gornto's heels. Suddenly the shadowy silhouette of the lieutenant became two silhouettes. The Japanese had stepped out to block his path. Desmond piled into the two scuffling forms, and bounced off to the side. He felt himself falling. He'd gone over the edge of the parapet. He and his equipment hit bottom with a thud. An agonizing pain shot through his left leg. It would not bear his weight.

But he couldn't stay there. The ammunition dump was nearby, with sentries posted. Dragging his leg behind him, announcing his identity in hoarse whispers, Desmond crawled to the dump, found a hole, and burrowed in. Feeling his leg with his fingers in the dark, he found that it was bleeding badly, and placed dressings on it to stop the blood. He could do nothing further, so he went back to sleep.

Dawn came. Desmond knew he should evacuate himself and his bad leg back to the battalion aid station. He could do his wounded buddies no good up here if his leg would not permit him to get to them. Yet he did not go. He was the only medic left, not just of Company B, but of the entire force at the escarpment. A medic with only one leg was better than no medic at all.

It was Saturday, May 5, the Sabbath. Breakfast over, he took his Bible and lesson pamphlet out of his pack and sat down, his back against a rock. For just a moment he allowed his thoughts to dwell on Dorothy, his parents, and his friends back home, going to church on a peaceful Sabbath far from the sounds of war. He did not envy them. By being here in this terrible place, he knew, he was doing his share to make it possible for them, and all Americans, to continue worshiping their God according to their own beliefs as a part of their heritage. He opened his lesson and began to read.

"How are things up on the hill?" The voice came from a full colonel standing above him. Desmond started to scramble to his feet, bad leg and all, but the colonel motioned him to stay where he was.

"I haven't been up there this morning, sir," Desmond said. "Our company CP is right over there, and you can check with them!"

The colonel nodded. "I want to see how our artillery is doing," he said, and proceeded on to the cargo nets.

Desmond turned back to his lesson. Several minutes went by. Then, from the top of the cliff, came the familiar cry, "Medic, medic!"

Desmond looked up at the men calling him. It was the Sabbath, and he had only one good leg. Nevertheless he answered, "What's the matter?"

"That colonel, the artillery spotter, he's been hit bad," the men shouted down.

Without thinking, Desmond grabbed his aid kits, jumped up, and started toward the cliff. His weight fell on his bad leg and it buckled under him. He went down, hard. Someone gave him a hand up.

"Oh, Lord, please help me," Desmond murmured. Again he put his weight on his bad leg. It held. One step, two, and then he realized that his bruised and wrenched leg was not paining him a bit. With his aid kits slung over his shoulders, he climbed the net to the top of the cliff, then carefully made his way toward the shell hole where the injured colonel lay.

Bullets whined over his head, and mortars and artillery shells burst on the hill. He paid no attention. By now he was used to the sound of death. He reached the shell hole and jumped in with the injured, unconscious colonel. A piece of shrapnel from a shell burst had shattered his arm and then ripped its way right on through his chest and back. He was bleeding heavily, and breathing through the hole in his chest. Desmond shouted to a man in the nearest shell hole to pass the word back that he needed blood plasma, and quick. He selected his largest battle dressings and tied them over the two large holes, front and back, to stop the gush of blood and the chest breathing.

He had finished the bandaging job when a soldier slid feet first into the hole with him. He had brought the blood plasma. Desmond inserted the large transfusion needle into a vein in the colonel's arm. In order for the plasma to drain from the container into the vein, it was necessary to hold it high. This meant exposing himself to the enemy just over the hill. Motionless, feeling naked, Desmond knelt there in full view of two armies, letting the life-giving plasma flow into the wounded man's vein. From behind, his men shouted at him to get down and fired across him to give him protection.

Another man skidded in with a litter. As Desmond held the container of plasma, the two men in the hole with him opened up the litter and eased the limp form onto it. The trip back toward the edge of the cliff, running, bent over, carrying the colonel, was a rough haul. The surgical dressings had slipped and the bleeding had commenced again. Desmond tied the dressings back. The transfusion needle had slipped out of the vein. Desmond tried to get it back in, but the vein had collapsed. He sent word to the battalion aid station that he had a colonel in serious condition and needed help. Captain Tann and Sergeant Howell appeared, but they were not able to get the needle back into the collapsed vein either.

"I think we'd better get him back to the hospital," Tann said. "We're not doing him any good here."

Four men picked up the litter and started carrying the colonel back toward the aid station. He died before he got there.

Desmond returned to his Sabbath School lesson. Again he was interrupted, this time by Captain Vernon.

"Doss," the captain said, "we have orders to move across the hill and take that pillbox no matter what the cost. Lieutenant Phillips is leading the attack. I know it is your Sabbath, and I know you don't have to go on this mission. But the men would like to have you with them and so would I."

"I'll go, captain," Doss said without hesitation. His Saviour had treated men on the Sabbath, and he could do no less. "But I'd like to finish my Sabbath School lesson first."

Captain Vernon opened his mouth to speak, then closed it again. He studied his company aid man for a moment. Doss's cotton uniform was dark brown and stiff with dried blood, the blood of the men whose lives he had saved and attempted to save. His eyes were sunk deep in their sockets with exhaustion. Vernon knew that he had seriously injured his leg and had nevertheless just gone out under fire to do his best to save a wounded man. How many men had Doss saved since this bloody battle had begun? The captain could not count them.

Vernon nodded agreement. "We'll wait for you."

Captain Vernon did not tell his company aid man that orders for this special mission had come down from 10th Army to Corps to Division to Regiment to Battalion to Company B. The entire American advance in Okinawa, a line several miles across and involving several divisions, was being held up by this one strong position. From the escarpment the Japanese dominated the terrain on either side. It could truly be said that the success of the Okinawa campaign rested on this mission.

And Captain Vernon delayed it so that one tired Sabbath keeper could read his Bible.

Not knowing he was holding up a war, Desmond reached the conclusion of the lesson. He closed his Bible, bowed his head and finished with a prayer. He stood up. Again his bruised leg miraculously supported him. "I'm ready when you are, captain."

The entire 1st Battalion was in on the attack, although Company B was to spearhead it. The company had been built up to well over 200 men for the Okinawa campaign, but after a week on the escarpment its fighting strength was down to 155 men.

These men were going into an even bigger battle than their worst fears, far bigger than the generals and their intelligence experts realized. None of them had any way of knowing that the entire Japanese strategy was keyed on this day. In every island battle prior to Okinawa, the Japanese had contested the Americans on the beachhead. This time their strategy was different. It was to permit the Americans to come onto Okinawa, all six divisions of them, unopposed. When the entire American force was on shore, a swarm of Kamikazes would be unleashed to sink the American fleet and cut off the supply lines. That would leave the forces stranded on the island.

The second step in their strategy was to wipe out those forces. The place chosen: A line anchored on the Maeda Escarpment, the most favorable terrain on the island for a counterattack. The time, that very day, May 5.

The first part of the program had failed; the Kamikazes had proved to be only a nuisance. But the second phase, the counterattack, was scheduled to go on nonetheless.

The high commands of two great forces, many miles apart, had chosen this very day to attack. Their point of contact was the escarpment. As the Japanese waited in their holes for zero hour, the Americans were beginning their advance. In the center was the 77th Division. At the apex of its attacking wedge the 307th Regiment, the First Battalion, Company B, and finally Lieutenant Phillips and his handpicked group of five volunteers. Their mission: The final assault on the big pillbox on the reverse slope of the hill.

The six men, covered by sweeping fire from the rear, crossed the broad top of the hill and crawled down the reverse slope toward the big hole. Each man carried a five-gallon can of gasoline. At Phillips's signal they removed the caps and tossed the cans in the hole. Phillips waited a moment, then tossed in a white phosphorus grenade. There was silence for a moment, then a mighty rumble. The entire hill shook.

Phillips and his men held on tight and looked at each other in wonder. This was more than they had expected. Far down beneath them an ammunition dump had obviously exploded. A few moments later the officers observing from the hills far to the rear across the valley and from the planes overhead saw a strange phenomenon. Puffs of white smoke came out of a hundred holes and crevices on top of the hill and from the slopes on all sides.

And out of many of those holes, even those on the American side, poured Japanese soldiers. They came running, screaming, firing rifles, and throwing grenades. This was the counterattack on which the Japanese pinned all their hopes. The whole thing reminded Desmond of hitting a hornet's nest with a stick, and seeing it erupt. The Americans met them head on. Captain Vernon brought every man up on the escarpment and the force dug in and held. But then the sheer weight of numbers and firepower, both from in front and from the rear, proved overwhelming.

At first there was the semblance of an orderly retreat, but then panic set in. Officers and noncoms were ranging up and down the hill shouting, threatening, trying to keep the men falling back in an orderly fashion. Some of the noncoms pointed their guns at their men, threatening to shoot anyone who fled. But panic and hysteria swept over the hilltop and the entire battalion, or what was left of it, began running back toward the cliff. Those men hit by enemy bullets and shells were left to lie where they had fallen, whether wounded or dead.

In the midst of this mad rush was the one remaining medic in the whole battalion, Desmond Doss. He ran from one fallen man to the other doing what he could. He didn't think of saving his own skin; he was too busy. He didn't think about the Japanese soldiers on the hilltop with him, shooting and throwing grenades. God had looked after him before. Why would He stop now? Trained as a medical soldier, seasoned by a hundred actions, secure in his conviction that when he was aiding his fellow men God was looking after him, Desmond Doss went calmly about his business of aiding the wounded, the only sane man on a hilltop mad with murder and fear.

Some of the other men, seeing him going about his business, were shamed into halting their pell-mell rush to the rear. Some gave him a hand with the wounded, helping them, dragging them to the edge of the cliff. But for hours it seemed to Desmond as though he was up there alone on top of the escarpment, raked by enemy fire, treating the wounded, pulling them back to the edge, then going back for more.

Those men who had been able to make their way down the cargo nets had collapsed and lay panting, regathering their breath and their senses. How long they had been there nobody really knew, when one of them happened to look up to the top of the cliff. He saw Desmond Doss standing there alone, the last unwounded man. The next thing the men at the bottom of the cliff knew, a litter with a wounded soldier strapped on it was being slowly lowered down the face of the cliff. Desmond had tied the man on it, had then taken a turn of the rope around the shattered stump of a tree, and was slowly paying out rope to permit the litter and its human burden to descend. A few feet from the bottom the rope securing the soldier to the litter slipped, and the unconscious man almost fell off. But a couple of men ran forward to steady the litter.

"Take him off!" Doss shouted down to them from above. "I've got more men up here. Send this one straight back to the aid station. Nonstop! He's bad off."

The men at the bottom untied the litter and removed the wounded man. They started to tie the litter back on to the rope, but Desmond stopped them.

"I don't want it," he called down. He had seen that first man nearly slip off and somehow, amidst all the confusion, his memory produced a picture in his mind. He remembered how he had tied a bowline in a double length of rope during mountain-climbing in West Virginia. Now he doubled the end of the rope and tied that bowline. The result was two loops, two loops that would not slip.

The area at the top of the cliff was covered with wounded men, conscious and unconscious. Desmond chose one of the men who seemed to be the most seriously injured. He slipped one of the man's legs through one of the loops of his bowline, the other leg through the other loop. Then he passed the rope around the man's chest and tied another bowline there. Now, holding on to the end of the rope, he gently rolled the wounded man over the edge of the cliff and, using the friction of the loop around the tree as a brake, let him down to the ground beneath.

"That man's seriously injured," he called down. "Get him back to the aid station nonstop!"

In that way, working alone, the only able-bodied man on the entire hilltop, Desmond lowered one man after another to safety and treatment beneath. He was partially protected by the slope and the rock wall, but as it was necessary for him to remain standing during several steps of the complete procedure, his head and shoulders were often exposed. Why did not Japanese bullets seek him out? Again Desmond accepted it as the beneficent will of his God.

Why did the Japanese, who had already chased the Americans back across the hilltop, not follow up their advantage? Only they knew. Perhaps the underground explosion had wreaked too great a toll for them to be able to mount their planned counterattack. Perhaps the artillery and mortar fire that Vernon called down on the top was sufficiently effective.

At any rate, Desmond remained on top of the cliff until he had lowered every wounded man to safety. How many men were there? No one counted. Only after it was all over and the full immensity of his actions began to sink in through the minds of the men who had witnessed it, did anyone begin to estimate the number. Captain Vernon and Lieutenant Gornto recalled that a total of 155 men had taken part in the abortive assault. They took a quick head count; only fifty-five men were on their feet at the base of the cliff. The difference—100 men—was the number they credited Desmond with saving.

He protested. "There couldn't have been more than fifty. It would have been impossible for me to handle any more than that."

"We'll split the difference with you," Captain Vernon proposed. "The official record will state seventy-five men saved by Pfc Doss."

Frightening and costly as the Japanese counterattack had been, it marked the last action on the escarpment. When the Japanese did not follow up their advantage, the Americans went back up on the hill and this time they stayed. The next day Company B, or what was left of it, was replaced with a fresh unit. Doss went back with them, tired to the very marrow of his bones.

Again Captain Tann and Sergeant Howell welcomed him. Tann looked at Desmond's uniform and shuddered. It was completely stiff and brown with dried blood and covered with flies.

"We're going to get you a new uniform," he promised.

Armies do not carry such luxuries as clean uniforms, even for such bloody campaigns as Okinawa; cargo space is taken up by such essentials as ammunition and food. But somehow fresh fatigues were found for the medic who had saved seventy-five men in one action. Desmond went back to the supply depot to get them. He scrubbed from the skin out, shaved, then put on his new uniform. If he'd had on a full-dress uniform he couldn't have been more impressive. An army photographer was rounded up to take a picture of a company aid man in a new uniform.

The commanding officer of the division, Major General A. D. Bruce, had heard of Desmond's heroism and wanted to talk to him personally. He came all the way up to the battalion aid station to see him. That was when Desmond was getting his new uniform.

Next day Desmond received an even greater present. It was a huge package from the States. Over the years Desmond had always listened to the Adventist radio program, *The Voice of Prophecy*. He had contributed to it for a long time. Following the Leyte campaign, in gratitude to the Almighty for sparing him during that bloody operation, Desmond sent in another contribution to *The Voice of Prophecy*. In this communication he asked Elder H. M. S. Richards, the Adventist evangelist who conducted the program, to send him some books for distribution among the company.

And now the books had arrived. Desmond got a big thrill out of unpacking them, passing them around to the men of the company. The number worked out perfectly. There was one book for every man, and one left over. The largest book was *The Great Controversy*, perhaps the most famous volume in the Adventist library, and Desmond presented it to the entire company to be kept in the field desk.

It was a fitting end to the battle of the escarpment. There was talk of another decoration to go with the Bronze Star he had won on Leyte. The officers wanted to recommend him for two Purple Hearts, one for the gash caused by the ricocheting rock, one for the injured leg. Although many

Doss in new fatigues given him to replace the uniform soaked with blood (U.S. Army Signal Corps photo).

# THE UNITED STATES OF AMERICA

TO ALL WHO SHALL SEE THESE PRESENTS, GREETING: THIS IS TO CERTIFY THAT THE PRESIDENT
OF THE UNITED STATES OF AMERICA AUTHORIZED BY EXECUTIVE ORDER, 24 AUGUST 1962 HAS AWARDED

## THE BRONZE STAR MEDAL

TO

CORPORAL DESMOND T. DOSS, UNITED STATES ARMY

FOR

meritorious service in connection with military
operations against the enemy on the Island of Leyto,
P.I., from December 7, 1944 to December 31, 1944.

GIVEN UNDER MY HAND IN THE CITY OF WASHINGTON
THIS 20th DAY OF February 19 86

*Mildred E. Hedberg*
THE ADJUTANT GENERAL

*John O. Marsh, Jr.*
SECRETARY OF THE ARMY

Bronze Star citation and certificate, one of two such awards
bestowed upon Doss for valor and bravery. (Courtesy Del E.
Webb Memorial Library, Loma Linda University, California.)

# THE UNITED STATES OF AMERICA

TO ALL WHO SHALL SEE THESE PRESENTS, GREETING:
THIS IS TO CERTIFY THAT
THE PRESIDENT OF THE UNITED STATES OF AMERICA
HAS AWARDED THE

## PURPLE HEART

ESTABLISHED BY GENERAL GEORGE WASHINGTON
AT NEWBURGH, NEW YORK, AUGUST 7, 1782
TO

CORPORAL DESMOND T. DOSS, UNITED STATES ARMY

FOR WOUNDS RECEIVED
IN ACTION
May 21, 1945    Okinawa
GIVEN UNDER MY HAND IN THE CITY OF WASHINGTON
THIS 13th DAY OF September 19 85

*Donald J. Delandro*
THE ADJUTANT GENERAL

*John O. Marsh, Jr.*
SECRETARY OF THE ARMY

Purple Heart citation and certificate, one of three such awards
for wounds Doss received in combat action. (Courtesy Del E.
Webb Memorial Library, Loma Linda University, California.)

a Purple Heart has been given for less, Desmond said one to cover both actions would be enough.

More important than a medal was the knowledge that he had been able to take care of the men he loved and send many of them back to their families.

It had been a busy Sabbath!

# CHAPTER 6

## THE LAST PATROL

After just two weeks of rest, Company B, with ninety-three replacements and several of the old men back after recovering from minor wounds and shock, returned to action. The few men who had been with it from the beginning might well have thought that by now they had seen everything. Yet a completely new type of action had been assigned them.

Captain Vernon took his key men, including Desmond, to the top of the hill known as Chocolate Drop, a mile or two past the escarpment, and pointed out the next hill. This would be their objective. Vernon's finger traced in the intervening valley a series of towers for a power line leading to the objective. Some had been knocked down.

"We'll guide on those towers," he said. "And it's a good thing we've got something to guide on, because this is going to be a night attack. The Japanese have been attacking at night all through the war. Well, we're going to give them a taste of their own medicine. We're going to pull out at 2:30 in the morning and hit that position before dawn."

As usual, the weather was cloudy with intermittent showers. There would be no moon that night. To enable each man to follow the one in front of him, Desmond handed out small gauze patches to be placed on the back of each man's pack. He hoped that the white spots could be seen in the dark.

Lieutenant Gornto had come down with pneumonia during the battle for the escarpment. A young officer replaced him. When the men started out through such utter darkness that they could not even see the white patch on the man in front of them, they had the chill feeling that this mission could not possibly end in anything but disaster. But such was the leadership of Captain Vernon that even the new men, who had known him for but a few days, followed with only a nominal amount of complaining.

They moved on through the torn-up terrain in a column of threes. The white squares might have been pitch black. They weren't visible. After several men had gotten lost, word was passed back for each man to hang on to the one in front of him. Occasionally flares went up, illuminating the valley in a harsh white light. Every man fell face down on his hands so that no white would show.

There was to be no sound. Rifles were emptied, bayonets attached. One Japanese soldier was encountered. Vernon gave one of his officers permission to put one shell in his carbine and use it.

Before long they had lost the path of the shot-up power structures. Frequent stops had to be made for the officers to check their compasses and to enable the men to catch up and get organized. But even then, as they neared the objective, the platoons became separated. No one will ever know for sure, but some of the men have always suspected that it was one platoon firing on another, rather than the Japanese, that gave their position away. No longer could they hope to make a surprise attack. The Japanese began throwing grenades. Two men were killed immediately. The rest sought cover.

More by feel than by sight, Desmond knew that the company had passed over the brow of a small hill and was proceeding down the back side when the shooting started. He and two riflemen stumbled into a shell hole and stayed there. One of the men grabbed Desmond by the arm. "Look!" came a hoarse whisper.

A Japanese soldier was silhouetted dimly against the skyline. He moved, and Desmond saw the sputtering fuse of a hand grenade coming straight to the shell hole. It landed right at his feet. The two other men were on the other side of the hole.

Instantaneously, by reflex action, like a farm boy getting close to a kicking mule, Desmond put his foot on the grenade. A split second later it exploded. He felt a jolt. It didn't hurt. Rather, it numbed him. He felt as though he was flying through the air head over heels. It knocked all the wind out of him. He shook his head and opened his eyes. He was still alive. The two men in the hole with him had gone, but the Japanese soldier was still there. Another grenade came sputtering through the night, but missed. Without thinking of how badly he was hurt, Desmond crawled out of that hole. Making his way through the underbrush, he called softly, over and over, "It's Doss, I'm hit." No one answered. He kept crawling until he was out of range of the grenades.

From far away he heard someone say that the company was withdrawing. He started crawling up the hill, dragging his left leg after him.

It was throbbing all the way down from hip to toe. He ran his hand along his thigh, down the calf. It was wet with blood all the way down. He realized that he had lost, and was still losing, a lot of blood, but he could not stop in the midst of the retreat to attend to himself. He felt himself passing out.

*What do you do for shock and loss of blood? You elevate the patient's feet.* Dutifully Desmond squirmed around so that he was lying with his head pointing downhill. He remained in that position until he felt the consciousness returning with the blood running into his brain. He began doggedly crawling up the hill again until he started blacking out, then turned around to lie with his head downhill.

Finally he reached the top of the hill and started down the other side. The first light of dawn was beginning to appear. He came to a shell hole.

"Who's there?" a voice whispered.

"Me, Doss."

"You're just the man I want to see," the soldier said. "I've been hit in the shoulder."

Working in the dim light, Desmond dressed the man's wounds. Then he checked himself. Reaching down into his trouser leg, he felt dried clots of blood, like pebbles. He pulled out a handful. But he couldn't work through his bloody trouser leg and he pulled his pants off. He felt down his left leg. Blood was running out of holes from his buttocks on down to his ankle. He could feel pieces of metal embedded in his flesh. He bandaged himself as best he could.

He knew he could crawl no further, and resigned himself to staying in the hole until daybreak. At least he had company. The hole was shallow, and he borrowed the soldier's shovel and tried to dig it out more. It was hard going and he gave up. He blacked out with his feet sticking out of the hole. When he opened his eyes it was light. He looked around him. The first thing he saw was a large artillery shell, unexploded, just inches from his head. He had been digging around it with the shovel. If he had hit it ... The thought of that knocked him into full consciousness.

The man with the shoulder wound had also lapsed into a coma, but Doss managed to rouse him. They decided to stay where they were and hope litter bearers would find them. Now Doss's wound was extremely painful. He took out a morphine syrette and showed the other soldier how to inject it. But the rifleman, squeamish about sticking the needle in the skin, squirted most of the morphine on his sleeve. Desmond finally gave himself the shot.

The company was beginning to pull itself together again. Desmond heard someone shout that Captain Vernon had been hit. He shouted back and started dragging himself in that direction. But Vernon came to him. Blood flowed out of the captain's mouth and dripped off his chin. A fragment of a hand grenade had passed through his mouth and out through his cheek.

"You have to go back, captain," Doss told him.

Captain Vernon gave a short little laugh. "I'm staying up here with my men, Doss," he mumbled through his torn mouth. Desmond knew it was useless to argue with him. He patched up the wound as best he could.

"Our artillery is going to drop a barrage on this area this morning," Vernon said. "We got to get word back to hold it."

But they had no communications. The company's radio was shot. Messengers were sent out. One located another unit with a functioning set, and they sent word to headquarters to call off the artillery.

In the meantime, of course, no litter bearers came into the area. Finally they arrived. One of them, T/5 Ralph E. Baker, knew Doss well. He immediately took over and quickly had his friend and fellow medic on the way back to the battalion aid station.

They had a long way to hike through a dangerous area on a day that had turned hot and muggy. Desmond drifted in and out of consciousness. He woke up with a jolt. Shells cracked through the trees. Enemy tanks fired in their direction. The four litter bearers had dropped to the ground, and Desmond had hit the dirt with them. The pain was agonizing, and it brought him completely to his senses. He looked around. Not ten feet away lay another wounded American soldier. Blood was all over his head, but he was breathing. Desmond instantly knew that this man's wound was more serious than his own.

When the shooting subsided and the four litter bearers got ready to proceed, Desmond rolled off the litter. "This man's hit in the head," he said. "You'd better take him."

Baker and the other three men protested vigorously. Desmond was their friend. "You're the one we started out with, Doss," Baker said. "We want to get you back safely."

"No, sir," Doss insisted. "You know that a head wound takes precedence. You get this man back. I can last a long time yet. Nobody knows how long this guy can last."

He finally convinced them. They rolled the unconscious man on the litter and left Desmond there alone. But before long someone else came along the trail. Doss recognized him immediately. He was Lewis Brooks from Richmond. He had been hit, but he could walk, and he offered to help Doss as best he could. Doss climbed to his feet and put his left arm around Brooks's neck. Brooks supported him with an arm around his waist. They started hobbling over the beat-up terrain toward the aid station.

Something hit Desmond's arm, the one around Brooks's neck, like a blow from a hammer. Instantly after he heard a rifle shot. Sniper! The bullet passed through Desmond's forearm and lodged in his upper arm. He knew it had broken the bones both above and below the elbow. But if it hadn't been for his arm it would have hit Brooks in the chest or throat. The two men hit the ground. They spotted a shell hole and wormed their way to it. Desmond had to hold on to his arm to keep it from flapping loosely. Crawling with one leg and two arms out of commission was not easy.

"What can we do?" Brooks wanted to know. "There aren't any medics to help you."

"You're all the medic I need."

"Who, me?" Brooks asked. "What can I do?"

"I'll show you. Give me the stock off your rifle."

Brooks took his rifle down and threw the barrel away. Desmond had left his aid kits back on a hill, but he still had his field jacket with him. He handed it to Brooks. "Here, wrap the stock in this. Now see if you can tear some strips off my shirt and tie my arm to it. Then tie the whole thing against my side."

Lying in the shell hole, Brooks managed to do it. Then they started out again. They could only hope that the sniper had moved on. Both of Desmond's wounds were now excruciatingly painful. The pieces of metal in his leg and buttocks—seventeen in all—cut his flesh and scraped against the bone whenever he moved his leg. He suffered from shock and loss of blood.

"I can't walk any farther," he suddenly told Brooks.

"Do you want to sit down?" Brooks asked.

Desmond thought about that a moment. Sit on what? That ripped and torn buttock? "No," he said.

"How about lying down, then?" Brooks asked.

Desmond could only shake his head. Things got blacker and blacker. He felt himself slowly crumpling to the ground.

# CHAPTER 7

## THE GREATEST HONOR

"**C**orporal," the voice behind him called. "Corporal Doss."

Desmond started, and pulled himself out of his reverie. Outside the hospital window the countryside of his beloved Virginia was beginning to turn red and brown and yellow with the colors of fall.

Desmond turned around, and began trying to stand at attention. Standing there was Colonel Hackett L. Connor, commanding officer of the hospital. He had a most uncolonel-like grin on his face.

"As you were, corporal!" he said, putting Desmond at ease. "Your promotion just came through and I thought I'd tell you about it myself."

"Thank you, sir," Desmond answered. In spite of the colonel's friendly tone, Desmond could not relax completely. He still found it hard to believe he was really here, home, safe, alive, near his loved ones, the war over. For months he had been living in a world of half blissful dream, half horrid nightmare. The war had gone on so long, so terribly long …

---

He had awakened at the battalion aid station. They'd given him a massive shot of morphine, and he went back into a fog. Then he found himself in a field hospital far behind the lines, sitting on an operating table. The pain was excruciating, both where he sat and where the doctors manipulated his broken arm.

"I can't sit down," he muttered. "It hurts."

"You have to. It's the only way we can get this cast on," one of the doctors insisted.

"I don't want to sit down," Doss murmured. He felt himself slipping into unconsciousness again. Suddenly a piercing odor went up his nose and his head cleared. Someone had broken an ammonia capsule under his nose.

Desmond in his extremely uncomfortable plaster cast. (Courtesy Del E. Webb Memorial Library, Loma Linda University, California.)

"You've got to stay awake," someone ordered.

Keeping him conscious with ammonia and conversation, the doctors and their assistants put a plaster cast on the entire upper part of his body. The cast held his arm out parallel with the ground, but bent at the elbow. When the plaster hardened, they finally let him get off his torn rear end. Then they could give him ether, and they put him under before they started extricating the jagged pieces of metal imbedded in his leg.

Later, in an ambulance, he bumped over an Okinawan road to the harbor where a hospital ship waited. A big, clumsy cast covered him from the waist to the neck. Bandages coiled around his ripped leg. What part of him was left was stark naked, under the GI blanket.

His Bible! *Where was Dorothy's Bible?* He felt for it with his good hand. It wasn't there.

At the dock he called the ambulance driver. "My Bible," he gasped. "I've lost my Bible!"

"Sure," soothed the driver. "They'll get you one on the ship."

"No, no!" Desmond cried, almost in hysterics. "I want *my* Bible, the one my wife gave me." He insisted that the driver pass the word to his friends at the battalion aid station, asking them to look for his Bible, his Bible with Dorothy's letter in it. In his agitation he didn't realize what a forlorn hope that was. You don't call off wars to search the jungle for a Bible!

Gradually he came around. His leg began to heal, although it would be some time before he could walk on it. The plaster cast was miserably uncomfortable, but Desmond knew he could live with it because he was going home.

The hospital ship took him to Guam. From there he was flown to Hawaii, where he remained for several impatient weeks. Inside the cast he felt filthy; he couldn't stand his own smell. He saw another patient in a light cast made of aluminum tubing.

"Why can't I have one of those?" he asked one of the ward attendants.

"Because yours is in fairly good shape," the attendant explained, and looked at his fellow medic meaningfully.

Desmond got it. He began working on his cast, soaking it, picking at it, and it didn't take him long to wreck it. He got his new, light, airplane splint.

Finally, two months after he'd been hit, he reached the United States. From Fort Lewis, Washington, he called Dorothy and heard her voice again for the first time in two years.

Each leg of the long journey home took an agonizingly long time. It was military policy to send each man as close to home as possible. Desmond wound up at the Army hospital at Swannanoa, North Carolina. His mother and father came to see him there.

Dorothy, however, had gone back to college and was within days of getting her degree. Desmond was promised a furlough as soon as he could get around, and he insisted that Dorothy stay on and graduate. By that time he could come to her.

Finally that day came. His arm stuck out clumsily in the crowded bus, and the granulated tissue in his leg wounds was painful, especially where he sat down.

But he was going home.

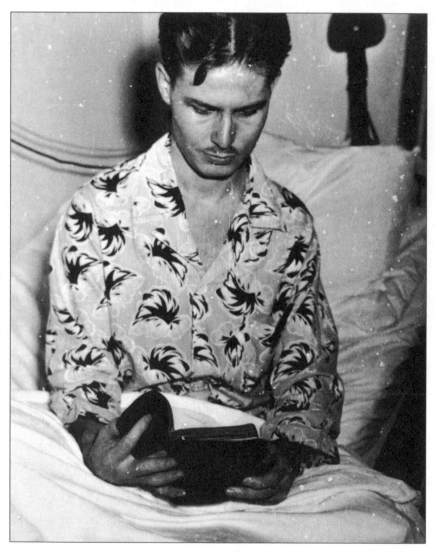

During convalescence from his wounds, Desmond reads the Bible his wife had given him. This Bible had accompanied him in three South Pacific combat campaigns, only to be lost on the Maeda Escarpment, and then found by members of his unit. (Courtesy Del E. Webb Memorial Library, Loma Linda University, California.)

Desmond had fought through three major campaigns, maintaining his composure and determination while others about him cracked from the strain. In a crowded bus station more than ten thousand miles from the fighting front, in the arms of his loved one, Desmond finally permitted the tears to course unashamedly down his cheeks. They were tears of joy.

Home at last and highly decorated for conspicuous gallantry and valor on the battlefield, Desmond and wife Dorothy celebrate with a reunion kiss. With the happy couple are Desmond's parents, Bertha and Thomas Doss. (Courtesy Del E. Webb Memorial Library, Loma Linda University, California.)

In the midst of this happiness he did not forget to thank the Lord above for deliverance from death. Out of his monthly pay he took a second tithe for his church, in gratitude for being permitted to return alive.

While at Swannanoa he received a warm and welcome letter from his friend Sergeant Howell in the medical battalion. All Desmond's old buddies sent their best. The division newspaper had published an exciting account of his heroism on the escarpment; Howell enclosed it. There was talk that Desmond was being recommended for a high decoration, perhaps even the Congressional Medal of Honor. One news item shocked and saddened him: Captain Vernon had been killed when a mortar shell scored a direct hit on the company command post.

And they had found Desmond's Bible! The whole company had turned out to look for it. Desmond saw, in his imagination, the green-clad soldiers fanning out, poking in shell holes, under debris, all the time keeping a sharp lookout for booby traps and snipers. He couldn't hold back the tears. To think that those men would do that for him! It could only mean that they felt for him the love and respect he felt for them.

Not only was the Bible hunt a great compliment and tribute to him, but he also gloried in the realization that this search for the Holy Bible surely brought those men closer to God.

The Bible was sent to Dorothy. Though waterlogged, with the cover falling off, it was still in reasonable condition, and later Desmond had it rebound. Tucked in its place was the lesson he had been working on, dated May 26, 1945. He had been wounded on May 21, a Monday.

When finally the bones had knit sufficiently so that the cast could be removed, the next stop was the Woodrow Wilson Hospital near Staunton, Virginia. Here he underwent an operation for removal of the bullet from his arm. At last the future seemed positive. It was early October 1945. The war was over, both in Europe and in Japan. The boys were coming home.

And here he was, *Corporal* Doss. "And that isn't all, corporal," Colonel Conner was saying. "I have a very great honor. I can inform you that you have been awarded the Congressional Medal of Honor, our country's highest honor."

"Sir?" Desmond asked. "Er, I mean—" His voice trailed off. The Congressional Medal of Honor, the nation's highest decoration, presented only to the nation's heroes for outstanding gallantry beyond the call of duty in actual combat. No sailor, no soldier, no marine, no general, no admiral could receive a greater award.

Through his mind raced a jumble of conflicting emotions. Gratitude, pride, vindication. He remembered that miserable night in the barracks at Fort Jackson when the Army shoes had come hurtling over the beds toward a scared young inductee on his knees in prayer. Now those men and others like them, officers and men he had served with in training and in battle, had recommended him for the nation's highest award.

There was sadness too, and grief. Desmond thought of Clarence Glenn, with the cheerful face that could smile no more; Herb Schechter, whose quiet, sincere voice would never be heard again; intrepid Captain Vernon, who had given his last order; all the other good buddies who had paid the supreme price.

Even at such a moment, Desmond Doss thought of others. They, he thought, were the ones who deserved that honor. And in keeping with his religious convictions, he thought too of the Power which had brought him through safely. He bowed his head and gave humble thanks to God.

The presentation of the medal was to be made at the White House, several days hence. A few days after Colonel Conner first told Desmond, he met him in the hall again. Desmond still had his Pfc stripe on.

"If I ever see that stripe on you again I'll rip it off myself," the colonel said. He sent a member of his staff, a lieutenant, to see to it that Desmond was outfitted with a complete new uniform and all the proper regalia. In addition to the corporal stripes on each arm, on his left arm he wore the Statue of Liberty patch of the 77th Division, two small gold horizontal stripes representing two six-month periods overseas, and a diagonal hash mark representing three years in the service. Over his left breast pocket he wore ribbons signifying the Bronze Star for valor, with cluster, the Purple Heart with two Oak Leaves, the Good Conduct Medal, the American ribbon with three bronze stars for the Asiatic-Pacific Campaign (Okinawa, Guam, and Leyte, with arrowhead for amphibious landing), and the Philippine Liberation with one star. Over this Christmas tree was the combat medic badge. Over his right shirt pocket he wore the small blue ribbon representing the Presidential unit citation given the 1st Battalion, 307th Infantry "for assaulting, capturing and securing the Escarpment."

Three days before the ceremony a member of the hospital staff brought Dorothy from Richmond to the hospital. The colonel furnished his official command car, with driver, for the 150-mile trip to Washington. Desmond was one of fifteen men to be awarded the medal in one ceremony on the White House lawn. For three days before that, however, they had the run of the town. Desmond and Dorothy, and Desmond's parents, stayed at the Willard Hotel, guests of the United States of America. They had a luxurious suite.

Each recipient had assigned to him an officer with practically unlimited funds for entertainment. The officer assigned to Desmond and Dorothy was enthusiastic and eager to please. He wanted to take them to nightclubs, to the best restaurants, to the liveliest places in town. He would go along, too, of course; it was not exactly an unpleasant duty.

Desmond, however, had learned from his Adventist friends that Elder Richards of *The Voice of Prophecy* was appearing at Sligo Church in

Takoma Park, a Washington suburb, the two nights before the ceremony. To Desmond, Elder Richards's preaching offered more than all the night-clubs, hot spots, and restaurants rolled into one. So his escort, a young Catholic officer who had been looking forward to painting the town red on an unlimited expense account, found himself in attendance at a Protestant evangelistic service two nights in a row.

Desmond and Dorothy finally permitted their escort to take them to a nightclub, after the services were over, and they had a miserable time. They didn't want a cocktail or highball, they didn't like the way the food was brought in dibs and dabs, they didn't enjoy the floor show, and the idea of spending all that money on such frivolity shocked them both. The sight-seeing tour of the city, however, including a boat ride down the Potomac to Arlington, proved most pleasant.

Then came the presentation ceremony. Desmond looked around at the other men gathered on the White House lawn. Thanks to his ideas of entertainment, he was unquestionably the freshest one there. One man showed up late with an obvious hangover.

Standing rigidly at attention, waiting to approach Harry S. Truman, the President of the United States, and receive a medal, then to receive the congratulations of General of the Army George Catlett Marshall, Desmond felt his knees shaking. One man after another stepped forward, heard his individual citation read by the President's aide, then as newsreel camera-men and newspaper photographers took his picture, received the medal and a handshake from the President. Desmond expected to be nervous, ill at ease, and embarrassed when he met President Truman.

His turn came. He walked forward and stopped, as rehearsed, at a line laid in the grass in front of the President. Truman obviously knew Doss's identity. He did something he had not done with the others. He stepped across the line, gave Desmond a hearty handshake, and made him feel at ease. The President held on to Desmond's hand all the time the citation was being read.

This is what Desmond heard:

Private First Class Desmond T. Doss was a company aid man with the 307th Infantry Medical Detachment when the 1st Battalion of that regiment assaulted a jagged escarpment 400 feet high near Orasoo-Mura, Okinawa, Ryukyu Islands, on April 29, 1945.

Doss was one of fifteen who received the Medal October 12, 1945, on the White House lawn. President Truman has his back to the camera. With him is Brigadier General Harry Vaughan, the president's military aide. Doss stands in the front row, second man to the left of President Truman (Associated Press).

President Truman awards Congressional Medal to
Doss. General Marshall watches. The autograph reads:
"Congratulations again to a Medal of Honor man. It is the
greatest of honors. Harry Truman to Desmond T. Doss."

President Harry S. Truman congratulates Corporal Desmond T. Doss after presenting Doss with the Congressional Medal of Honor on October 12, 1945. (Courtesy Del E. Webb Memorial Library, Loma Linda University, California.)

As our troops gained the summit, a heavy concentration of artillery, mortar, and machine-gun fire crashed into them, inflicting approximately seventy-five casualties and driving the others back. Private Doss refused to seek cover and remained in the fire-swept area with the many stricken, carrying them one by one to the edge of the escarpment and there lowering them on a rope-supported litter down the face of a cliff to friendly hands.

On May 2, he exposed himself to heavy rifle and mortar fire in rescuing a wounded man 200 yards forward of the lines on the same escarpment; and two days later he treated four men who had been cut down while assaulting a strongly defended cave, advancing through a shower of grenades to within eight yards of enemy forces in a cave's mouth, where he dressed his comrades' wounds before making four separate trips under fire to evacuate them to safety.

On May 5, he unhesitatingly braved enemy shelling and small-arms fire to assist an artillery officer. He applied bandages, moved his patient to a spot that offered protection from small-arms fire, and, while artillery and mortar shells fell close by, painstakingly administered plasma. Later that day, when an American was severely wounded by fire from a cave, Private Doss crawled to him where he had fallen twenty-five feet from the enemy position, rendered aid, and carried him 100 yards to safety while continually exposed to enemy fire.

On May 21, in a night attack on high ground near Shuri, he remained in exposed territory while the rest of his company took cover, fearlessly risking the chance that he would be mistaken for an infiltrating Japanese and giving aid to the injured until he was himself seriously wounded in the legs by the explosion of a grenade. Rather than call another aid man from cover, he cared for his own injuries and waited five hours before litter bearers reached him and started carrying him to cover.

The trio was caught in an enemy tank attack and Private Doss, seeing a more critically wounded man nearby, crawled off the litter and directed the bearers to give their first attention to the other man. Awaiting the litter bearers' return, he was again struck, this time suffering a compound fracture of one arm. With magnificent fortitude he bound a rifle stock to his shattered arm as a splint and then crawled 300 yards over rough terrain to the aid station.

Through his outstanding bravery and unflinching determination in the face of desperately dangerous conditions Private Doss saved the lives of many soldiers. His name became a symbol throughout the 77th Infantry Division for outstanding gallantry far above and beyond the call of duty.[5]

"I'm proud of you," the President said. "You really deserve this. I consider this a greater honor than being President." Then he hung the medal, the nation's highest honor, around Desmond's neck.

The United States Army version of the Congressional Medal of Honor. (Courtesy Del E. Webb Memorial Library, Loma Linda University, California.)

---

5    Though the events described in the citation are of course true, they were based on the hasty recollections of men immediately following the actions described, and their sequence is not in exact order.

General George C. Marshall congratulates
Medal winner Desmond T. Doss.

After that, General Marshall came down the line and congratulated the medal winners. This was another thrill. Desmond had carried that document signed by Marshall, stipulating he would not be forced to bear arms, all during the war.

The War Department had put out a full press release on Desmond's being awarded the medal. His escort obtained several copies of it, and Desmond and Dorothy and their parents read it together:

A conscientious objector who was assigned to the Medical Corps, United States Army, Private First Class Desmond T. Doss, of Lynchburg, Virginia, displayed such outstanding bravery and unflinching determination in aiding his wounded comrades in the fierce Okinawa campaign that he has been awarded the Medal of Honor, it was announced today by the War Department.

The Nation's highest decoration goes to the twenty-six-year-old soldier who, although not bearing arms, performed so many feats of heroism on the battlefields of Guam, Leyte, and Okinawa that his name became a symbol for outstanding gallantry throughout the 77th Infantry "Statue of Liberty" Division.

Private Doss's wife, Dorothy Pauline, lives at Route 9, Box 66, Richmond, Virginia; and his parents, Mr. and Mrs. William T. Doss, reside at 1835 Easley Avenue, Lynchburg.

The medal will be presented to Private Doss by President Truman at the White House on Friday, October 12.

Private Doss, a member of the 307th Infantry Medical Detachment, 1st Battalion, received the unstinting praise of fighting men of the 77th Division from generals to privates.

Brigadier General Edwin H. Randle, commanding general of the division, asserted, "This soldier by his unfailing devotion to duty and his gallantry and intrepidity at the risk of his life above and beyond the call of duty has gained the respect, admiration, and affection of the entire division."

This is the more noteworthy as, on being inducted into the military service, Private Doss was, and still is, a conscientious objector. He refused to carry arms or even touch a weapon. His organization commander transferred him to the battalion medical detachment where he was made company aid man because he wanted to be forward with the men.

In the Guam and Leyte campaigns Private Doss demonstrated the same qualities. No matter how heavy the fire, he remained and cared for wounded men regardless of consequences or danger.

Private Doss was awarded the Medal of Honor for specific acts of supreme heroism on Okinawa in the Ryukyu Islands between April 29 and May 21, 1945.

First Lieutenant Onless C. Brister, 245 Central Avenue, Winona, Mississippi, pointed out, "Private Doss was at all times up with the front lines to care for injured men. In several instances he braved intense enemy small-arms and mortar fire to give aid and to move men who were wounded."

First Lieutenant Cecil L. Gornto, of Live Oak, Florida, was 1st Platoon leader of Company B to which Private Doss was attached from April 29 to May 8.

"On the morning of April 29," Lieutenant Gornto related, "heavy mortar fire was falling in the area, and someone called for a medic. Private Doss left his hole and climbed to the top of the hill. He found the wounded man in total darkness and gave him first aid. As soon as it was light enough, I observed him lowering the wounded man over the cliff on a rope to evacuate him. This man had both legs blown off."

Another link in the Doss chain of sterling heroism was told by Second Lieutenant Kenneth L. Phillips, Route 3, Lexington, North Carolina.

Citation and certificate for the Congressional Medal of Honor presented to Desmond T. Doss. (Courtesy Del E. Webb Memorial Library, Loma Linda University, California.)

"On May 5, during an intense grenade battle in the vicinity of Kakazu," Lieutenant Phillips said, "four men were badly wounded while trying to blow up a cave. They were lying under a vicious hail of grenade and mortar fire. With total disregard for his own personal safety, Private Doss went forth four times and pulled the wounded men to safety."

Private First Class Carl B. Bentley, of Fulshear, Texas, spoke of an instance on May 2.

"Private Doss was told of a man out in the front lines between our line and the Japs. He went out and brought this man in under very heavy rifle and knee-mortar fire."

The climax in the Virginian's amazing battle career as a male angel of mercy occurred on the night of May 21, when he was badly injured, thereby winning an Oak Leaf Cluster to the Purple Heart he earned May 10, when he was less seriously wounded. Technician Fifth Grade Ralph E. Baker, of the 1st Battalion medics, tells the story.

"On May 21, Private Doss was wounded by an enemy grenade. Instead of calling another aid man from the safety of his foxhole, Private Doss treated his own wounds and gave himself a shot of morphine when the pain became too great.

"Litter bearers reached him in the morning, almost six hours later. After they carried him about fifty yards, the litter bearers were halted momentarily by bursts of mortar fire. Private Doss crawled off the litter and told the aid men to take more seriously wounded men in first.

"He was wounded a second time while he lay there. He bound a rifle stock to his shattered arm to form a splint and crawled to the aid station despite his wounds."

Private Doss, who was born February 7, 1919, in Lynchburg, entered the Army at Camp Lee, Virginia, on April 1, 1942. He was a ship joiner before his induction. He was awarded the Bronze Star for his meritorious service as a medical aid man on Leyte in the Philippine Islands from December 7 to 21, 1944.[6]

---

6    Again there are small discrepancies.

To top it all, Desmond was given a ten-day furlough. He and Dorothy went to her home in Richmond. For weeks he had been trying to get transferred to the McGuire General Hospital there. He was now able to get around fairly well. His leg was almost as good as new, except for a few small fragments of metal which remained in it and occasionally caused pain. The bones in his shattered arm had knit, the bullet had been removed, and the incision was healing well. Desmond had been told that he would not be able to use the arm again, but he believed that with God's help and his own continued effort and exercise he would develop strength and mobility in it.

Major General A. D. Bruce autographed this picture, "To Desmond T. Doss, Medal of Honor, an outstanding godly hero of the 77th Division." (U.S. Army Signal Corps photo.)

Following the presentation, Dorothy Doss
beamed proudly at her husband.

In the near future he would receive his honorable discharge. He had not yet decided whether he would arrange to be discharged out of the special provisions granted a winner of the Congressional Medal of Honor, as a disabled veteran, or on the basis of the large number of discharge points he had earned overseas and in combat.

Pending his separation from the service, it would be a great convenience if he could be stationed at McGuire, to be near Dorothy. One day he dropped in to the hospital to ask if he could in any way expedite the transfer from Woodrow Wilson. Papers throughout the country, indeed all over the world, had carried the story of the conscientious objector who had won the Congressional Medal of Honor. In Richmond, because of Dorothy's connection with the city, the papers had devoted large spreads to the hero-medic. When he entered the administration building, he was recognized immediately and escorted into the office of the commanding officer.

"You don't need to have a transfer," Desmond was told. "You don't even have to go back to Woodrow Wilson. We'll send word back there you weren't feeling well and checked in with us while you were here on furlough."

"Oh, no," Desmond said, unused to cutting corners in the military, "I'll go back there and check out personally."

In the meantime Desmond had to make another appearance. His hometown, Lynchburg, was clamoring for him to come back for a hero's welcome. Plans were quickly made. He was met at the station by city officials and driven down Main Street in an open car in a full military parade. Bands played and banners proclaimed him the "Wonder Man of Okinawa." Post 16 of the American Legion gave him a life membership.

Late in October, Desmond returned to Woodrow Wilson to make his transfer. Colonel Conner met him with a big salute. When Desmond looked embarrassed the colonel said, "Remember, soldier, the Medal of Honor rates the salute of a five-star general." [7]

And so Desmond returned to McGuire, in Richmond. He had a Class A pass, which meant that he could come and go as he liked. He had long been thinking about what he would like to do when he got out of the service. Though some strength was beginning to come back to his left arm, he knew he would not be able to go back to his old trade of carpentry, or, indeed, any craft which required two good arms. He was exploring, however, two interesting avenues of financial fulfillment.

While at Swannanoa Hospital he had spent a weekend at the home of a friend who was a florist. The friend had had to make a few wreaths, and Desmond had helped. He was pleased with the wreath he had made; he thought it as good as that made by the professionals.

Desmond had always loved flowers. As a child, then as a youth, he had cultivated flowers and flowering shrubs. Now there was much talk of the GI Bill of Rights which would help veterans in their adjustment to peace. Perhaps, Desmond thought, the new legislation would in some way make it possible for him to learn more about flowers and the florist business, and perhaps even have his own florist shop.

---

7   This is a common misconception. Many high officers salute Medal of Honor winners, but it is a matter of individual choice, not a requirement. Regulations did, in 1945, provide that a Medal of Honor man may travel in a military aircraft when space is available, that his son may get special assistance with an appointment to West Point or Annapolis, that he would receive $2 per month and a pension of $120 a year at the age of 65.

The other avenue was also concerned with living, beautiful organisms, though somewhat different from flowers. In Richmond one day he passed a small shop featuring tropical fish, and he became interested in them. The proprietor appreciated his interest and whetted it. A man could earn a comfortable and pleasant living raising and selling exotic fish, he said.

Surely now Desmond would, in the words of the ninety-first psalm, "abide under the shadow of the Almighty." His Army pay and allotment continued. He wore the nation's highest decoration.

At long last he and Dorothy could begin to raise that family of which they had dreamed so many years. They both loved children. They were young and brave and positive that they could provide for those children in a Christian home.

Desmond Doss, first wife Dorothy (Schutte) Doss and his mother Bertha (Oliver) Doss pose in front of the World War II barracks at an unknown Army base after his extended hospitalization for wounds received in Okinawa, but before his discharge from the Army. (Courtesy Del E. Webb Memorial Library, Loma Linda University, California.)

If it were possible to make Desmond's faith in God any stronger, to increase his desire to serve the Lord and his fellow man and to spread the gospel, then his ordeal in the South Pacific had done just that. Too many times he had crossed areas exposed to small-arms, mortar, even artillery fire on an errand of mercy without being scratched, not to believe that the Lord was protecting him. He had been wounded, yes, and seriously so, but he was alive, and home, and healthy—and he was thankful.

He further resolved that, as a tribute and in gratitude to the glory of God, he would go anywhere the church asked him, speak to whatever group wanted to hear him, and in any and every way advance the work of the Lord and the church.

# CHAPTER 8

## PEACE AND ADVERSITY

I t would be wonderful to leave Desmond and Dorothy at that moment in time where they were at the zenith of their happiness, together, looking ahead to the future they had dreamed of through four difficult years. Indeed, many friends, acquaintances, and fellow members of the Seventh-day Adventist Church over the world, have taken it for granted that Desmond and Dorothy have led a contented and uneventful life since the war.

Unfortunately, they have met with some adversities. Just before Desmond planned to be separated from the Army, he was examined for what he thought must be a touch of pleurisy. The diagnosis: *tuberculosis*. The sound of the dread word numbed him. Later, in discussing his previous medical history with the doctors, he recalled that period on Leyte when he had chills and fever and was so weak he could not keep up with the company. That had been the beginning of it. Then came the Maeda Escarpment with its hot days, cold, wet nights, lack of sleep, exhaustion, and long periods without proper food.

Even then it could have been worse. The disease was restricted to one lung. The doctors hoped it could be cleared up easily.

Instead of being discharged and settling down to live happily ever after with Dorothy, Desmond was shipped two thousand miles away from her, to Fitzsimmons General Hospital in Denver, Colorado. "It's the best," the doctors told him, "and you deserve the best."

Lonely, almost forgotten, depressed, Desmond sank lower and lower. He worried about Dorothy, now pregnant with the child they had waited for so long. The doctors felt that he would make a quicker recovery if there were no stimulation whatsoever, not even that of his beloved wife, and they remained apart, miserably apart. These two people did not belong apart. Finally Desmond convinced the doctors that his progress could not possibly be slower, and Dorothy was permitted to come to him. She lived with an Adventist family in Denver and visited Desmond every day. He began improving immediately.

When he seemed much better, Desmond was discharged from the Army and transferred, as a veteran with full benefits, to McGuire Hospital in Richmond, now a veterans' facility. It was an unfortunate move. The hospital administration, adjusting to civilian military control, permitted some laxness. One tragic example was unlimited smoking. Even patients in advanced stages of tuberculosis smoked like chimneys. Desmond saw men smoke themselves to death, and sometimes the smoke around him was so thick that he was afraid he would join them.

Nothing could be worse than that environment, and Desmond talked the powers that be into permitting him to leave the hospital as an outpatient. He and Dorothy went home to Lynchburg. He had a weekly treatment in which air was injected into his left pleural cavity to collapse the lung and permit it to rest. Desmond himself was under orders to rest during a large part of every day. He had been warned not to do any work requiring physical exertion.

But now Desmond had not only himself and Dorothy to feed, but also Desmond Thomas Doss, Jr., born September 15, 1946. The baby was not permitted to come near his father lest he be infected. Desmond's total pension, for 100 percent disability, was $118 a month. Dorothy worked in a hosiery mill from three to eleven p.m. The American Legion in Lynchburg had helped get him a priority for a new car so he could get to the doctor for the pneumo-thorax treatment, and Desmond had been too appreciative of their efforts to say he couldn't afford it. So he had payments to keep up.

His friend in a Richmond fish shop sold him a complete set-up for raising tropical fish at cost, along with breeding stock of such exotics as black mollies, angelfish, swordtails, guppies, and snails. It was a good deal, in an enterprise which can be highly profitable. He bought books and plunged into the operation on a large scale. Desmond is incapable of doing anything in a small way.

One day, checking the thermometer, he noted that the reading was too low. He quickly began raising the temperature of the water to the required point. Still the mercury in the thermometer did not rise. Not until after he had lost every single fish did he discover that the fault lay in the thermometer.

He was out of the fish business completely. He had started too big. He had nothing left with which to begin again. He had already been doing too

Dorothy and Desmond Doss with son Desmond T.
(Tommy) Doss, Jr. (Courtesy Del E. Webb Memorial
Library, Loma Linda University, California.)

much, working with the fish and about the yard. Now, in a desperate effort to get some money in, he began selling door-to-door in the neighborhood.

Activity, pressure, anxiety. At one of his checkups the doctor examined him through a fluoroscope. After a long pause he said, "Desmond, I can't treat you here anymore."

Now he had tuberculosis in both lungs. This time it was the VA's Oteen Hospital near Asheville, North Carolina. His condition steadily worsened. Finally Dorothy and little Tommy moved to Asheville to be near him. From then on his condition improved.

Doss holds the bent bullet that passed through his forearm and lodged against the bone in his upper arm, later to be removed by army surgeons. (Gordon Engen)

Desmond, Jr. ("Tommy") admires his
father's Congressional Medal.

The doctors had now decided that the left lung must be removed. However, before removing it, they had to build it up so that it could take some of the load off the right lung, thus permitting the right lung to heal. The left lung, however, was in such bad shape that the bronchial tubes had a tendency to collapse. They had to be dilated. This was done every two weeks, physically, in a modern scientific torture called bronchoscopy. In the bronchoscopy a chrome pipe the size of a man's thumb is pushed down the throat so that forceps can be inserted to dilate the tubes. It is extremely painful. After every treatment Desmond would spit blood for days. It tore him up; he couldn't eat. And he had more than thirty bronchoscopies over a period of a little more than a year.

In early 1950 he received his reward: Two operations. In the first stage, the left lung plus one and a half ribs on the left side were removed. A month later four and a half more ribs were removed. A year later he had recovered to the point that he could be sent to Swannanoa for rehabilitation. Dorothy, of course, and little Tommy came along too, living in a furnished room in town. The only work that permitted her both to take care of Tommy and visit Desmond was part-time housecleaning.

Tommy Doss on his fourth birthday
(Dunbar-Stanley Studios).

Desmond was released from Swannanoa in October 1951. Since being wounded more than six years before, he had spent only a few months out of a hospital. His only income had been the monthly check, now $138, he received from his grateful government, and the few dollars Dorothy made in domestic work.

Desmond looked first for some kind of work in Richmond, but no one wanted a Medal of Honor winner with a shot-up leg, a withered arm, and only one lung. He went on to Lynchburg. There he arranged for on-the-job training as a cabinetmaker, for which he would be paid out of the GI Bill of Rights. Desmond gradually came to realize that his physical condition would not let him work all day, every working day. Yet it was required of him. He lived in constant fear that if he did not work he would lose his income, and that if he did work he would suffer a relapse and have to go back to the hospital.

They were renting an old farmhouse outside of Lynchburg for $50 a month. It was impossible to heat and so shabby that Desmond offered to paint it if the landlord would furnish the paint. The landlord agreed—and Desmond found that the paint was mostly used motor oil.

In addition to little Tommy, now five years old, Dorothy took care of her sister's two children.

Desmond nailed together this cabin on Lookout Mountain, Georgia, when the family's fortune was at ebb tide. (Courtesy Del E. Webb Memorial Library, Loma Linda University, California.)

That summer of 1952 the program committees of Adventist camp meetings in several parts of the country asked Desmond to come and tell of his experiences in which he won the nation's highest award. Desmond had never refused a speaking engagement provided he was out of the hospital or could get out. It was his unilateral agreement with God. Though he felt inadequate as a public speaker, he learned to overcome his nervousness.

The contented couple relax in the porch swing of their modest country home, Rising Fawn, Georgia, near Chattanooga, Tennessee (circa 1967).

Because it was easier to show people than to tell them, he carried with him a length of rope and demonstrated the double bowline with which he lowered the wounded from the escarpment. He showed the Bible and the Medal of Honor. His presentation became effective, even appealing. He was, after all, one of the nation's great heroes, and the only conscientious objector to win the Congressional Medal of Honor. If he had just stood up there without speaking, he would have been an attraction.

Desmond demonstrates the double bowline knot
he discovered, and the rope sling he used to lower
seventy-five wounded from the escarpment.

His homely, hesitant little speech, his demonstration with the rope, and, finally, his unashamed and unassuming faith in his Creator have surely combined to encourage thousands of persons to reaffirm their own belief in the God of Desmond Doss.

Later that year Dorothy collapsed. She had held herself together for nine years of married life, a year of living in the catch-as-catch-can housing around Army camps, two years while the man she loved served in the bloody South Pacific, and now six years of strain and hardship. No one could blame Dorothy Doss for breaking down.

After some months of sporadic and unsatisfactory treatment, Desmond took Dorothy to the little Seventh-day Adventist sanitarium near Wildwood, Georgia. Here, at last, with patience, love, faith, understanding, and prayer, Dorothy began to recover. Desmond was caring for Tommy as best he could, and working in a maintenance capacity for a small, poor institution for young children on top of rugged, rocky Lookout Mountain just a few miles from Wildwood. It was a comfortless, penny-pinching existence. He managed to acquire a small four-acre tract of land with a trailer on it for $50 an acre and, in his spare time, put together a small frame house of the materials bought at bargains here and there. The money came from cashing in his Government life insurance.

In 1957 Desmond was asked to fly to Hollywood, California, all expenses paid, to discuss a possible movie. When he arrived, he was whisked to a studio and then, suddenly, out on a stage in front of an audience of several hundred people. He was on the television program *This Is Your Life.* For the next half hour he saw his life in review. Colonel Cooney had flown in from Florida to say how he had seriously considered sending Private Doss back from Hawaii because he wouldn't carry a gun. Officers and men of B Company told how Desmond had saved their lives, and how his actions that day on the escarpment were the most heroic thing they had ever seen. Dorothy and Tommy were there too, and his mother and father. At the end of the show, Ralph Edwards, the master of ceremonies, presented him with a power saw, a power shop, movie camera, money enough to increase his little holding on Lookout Mountain to seven acres, a cow, tractor with attachments, and a station wagon.

That marked the beginning of the upturn in the life of Desmond, Dorothy, and Tommy Doss. Desmond has been able to make his house solid and comfortable. He grows the vegetables and fruits he likes. There's a small lake, with a boat, ducks, and fish. His disability payments have increased,

Ralph Edwards, producer of "This Is Your Life,"
inscribed picture, "To Desmond—one of God's
great guys—with friendship and admiration."
(This Is Your Life® Photo of Desmond Doss
courtesy of Ralph Edwards Productions.)

and in 1965, Congress passed a law paying Medal of Honor winners $100 extra a month.

Desmond enjoys his leisure moments
spent at a small lake near home.

Dorothy went back to school and got her nursing degree. However, in 1966 she began the intensely satisfying work of teaching in the Head Start program.

And little Tommy is little Tommy no longer. At the age of twenty he was inducted into the Armed Services. Like his father before him, but with none of the confusion, he was placed in the medical department where he belonged and where he wanted to be. However, also like his father before, Tommy fell in love and got married. He and his wife decided it would be more practical for him to accept the special discharge available to only sons of deceased or war-disabled veterans.

For many years of Tommy's life Desmond could not be the father he wanted to be. A memory that haunts him still is of his baby crawling to the threshold of his room in the little house in Lynchburg, and stopping there. It was a household rule that the baby could not enter his tubercular father's room, and that the father could not come near his son. Then there were the many years in which either Desmond or Dorothy was in a hospital.

With customary enthusiasm, Doss has worked to
build a Seventh-day Adventist church and school—
"The greatest undertaking of my life," he says.

Unable to help his own child, Desmond in recent years has found a way
to help others. With his own money and labor, and that of others in the
community, he set out to enlarge the little church on Lookout Mountain
to include a school for the children of the mountain. It is a poor region,
with played-out coal mines and small, scrubby farms. Money does not
come easily. But under the inspirational, hardworking leadership of Desmond Doss, who has done far more than he has asked anyone else to do,
people have contributed both their goods and their energies. One church

member, convalescing from a long illness and unable to work, sold his own home in order to make a contribution.

"The Lookout Mountain Seventh-day Adventist Church and school is the greatest undertaking of my life," Desmond said.

Desmond continues to serve his country as leader of Rescue Service of the Civilian Defense, Area 4, Walker County, Georgia. Doss is in front row, next to right. Chief of Walker County Rescue Service is Lee Henry. (Courtesy of the Chattanooga Times Free Press.)

As the recipient of a monthly stipend from the government, Desmond has sought to serve his country and his people as best he could in return. When the Civilian Defense rescue service was formed in Walker County, Georgia, Desmond was the leader in his area. He helped buy an old truck, and he put in long hours and considerable money helping to fix it up and equip it.

In April 1966, his squad was put to the test: Eight boy scouts and three adult leaders became lost in a cave. Working around the clock in the dark, wet, gas-filled cavern, Desmond and his co-workers saved seven of the scouts and one of the leaders. After it was all over, the other rescue workers revealed that Desmond spent more consecutive hours in the cave, working harder, than anyone else.

And it was the Sabbath too.

# CHAPTER 9

## THE HERITAGE OF DESMOND DOSS

Twenty years after Desmond Doss was awarded the Medal of Honor, another patriotic young American went out to serve his country on the battlefield. His name was Curtis A. Reed, of Gillette, Wyoming. Like Desmond, he was a Seventh-day Adventist. Like Desmond, he was willing and eager to serve his country.

Unlike Desmond, who joined a newly reactivated division, Reed became a part of the famous 1st Division, the Big Red One. The division was already in service in the Republic of Vietnam when Curtis Reed joined it. The other men in the headquarters company, 1st Battalion, 26th Infantry, saw that he had no gun, and they quickly learned that he was a Sabbath keeper. But how different was his reception from that of Desmond Doss twenty years before!

"Boy," one of the veterans of the Vietnam campaign said, with admiration, "I'd never have the nerve to go out on one of these missions without a gun."

"You medics have got a lot more guts than I have," said another rifleman.

From the beginning a warm feeling of camaraderie developed between Reed and the men whose lives he someday might save. That day came March 24, 1966, in the jungles north of Phu Loi.

Reed's company was advancing slowly through the dense underbrush of a fortified area when grenades began bursting all around them, and bullets whistled through the thicket. The Americans hit the ground and lay still.

All except Curtis Reed. Wounded men were calling out. He moved forward in the direction of both his wounded men and the Viet Cong. The first casualty was a good friend, a sergeant, hit in the shoulder. Reed cut away the upper part of the man's jacket and applied a battle dressing. The sergeant kept telling him to go attend to the other men, but Reed insisted on first stanching the flow of blood.

He crawled on farther, past a dead soldier who had been shot in the head, to another sergeant who had been badly hit. The soldier died while Reed was working on him. Meanwhile another medic came up and began treating another wounded American. He rose up on his knees, and instantly five shots rang out. He was hit three times in the chest, twice in the leg. The unseen Viet Cong were so close Reed smelled the acrid gunpowder. Reed did what he could for his fellow medic, but the wounds were fatal.

The next man had been hit twice, in the head and in the leg. Reed treated him and continued. He was wet with blood and sweat. The heat was intense, and the humidity in the breathless jungle was extremely enervating. But Reed kept moving, crawling to his buddies and treating them. Finally tanks came up to cover the company's retreat. Curtis Reed was the last man to leave the bloody area.

For his heroism in that operation the young Adventist was awarded the Bronze Star and later the Oak Leaf cluster "for distinguishing himself by outstanding meritorious service in connection with ground operations against a hostile force. ..."

> "Through his untiring efforts and professional ability, he consistently obtained outstanding results," the citation continued. "He was quick to grasp the implications of new problems with which he was faced as a result of the ever-changing situation inherent in a counter-insurgency operation and to find ways and means to solve those problems. The energetic application of his extensive knowledge materially contributed to the effort of the U.S. mission to the Republic of Vietnam to assist that country in ridding itself of the Communist threat to its freedom.

> "His initiative, zeal, sound judgment, and devotion to duty have been in the highest tradition of the United States Army and reflect great credit on him and on the military service."

It is interesting to note that in that citation there is no mention of the fact that Reed was a conscientious objector or Seventh-day Adventist. He was simply an American soldier, doing his job in a distinguished, outstanding manner.

Many of the more than 7,000 Adventist soldiers in the Army today report that they are accepted as they are and for what they are without any critical comment. The individual actions of these brave men have done much to make them welcome in the military establishment.

At the one hundredth anniversary celebration of the creation of the
Congressional Medal, World War II Medal winners chose Doss to represent
them at the observances. Doss had a long chat with President Kennedy.
(Courtesy Del E. Webb Memorial Library, Loma Linda University, California.)

However, there is no question but that having a Congressional Medal
of Honor winner in their number has made military service easier for the
thousands of young Adventists who have proved their willingness and
eagerness to serve their country in uniform.

There is a great reverence among military men for the nation's highest
award, the Congressional Medal of Honor. Those men who have won it
have organized their own group which meets in convention with respectful cooperation from the Armed Services in the host city once a year. Desmond has attended every convention his health has permitted. He enjoys
the respect of his fellow heroes. On the 100th anniversary of the creation of

the medal, in 1962, it was Desmond who was selected by his fellow Medal winners of World War II to represent them at the White House. He and President Kennedy had a pleasant chat.

At the inauguration of Camp Doss, Michigan, Desmond appears with Brig. Gen. Floyd Wergeland, Pastor Carlyle B. Haynes, and Dr. Everett N. Dick.

As the only conscientious objector to win the medal he is always sought out by the local press, radio, and television at convention cities for special interviews and appearances. He is frequently sought for television shows. Millions of people, especially those who have come of age during the generation following World War II, have learned about the Seventh-day

Adventist Church and its patriotic policy of cooperation with its government through its war hero, Desmond Doss.

Medical cadets receive preinduction military training at Camp Doss.

During the Korean War, the War Services Commission of the Seventh-day Adventist Church decided to establish a permanent national training camp for future medical soldiers. Carlyle B. Haynes, chairman of the commission, the one who had done so much to help Desmond during his early service in World War II, and Everett N. Dick, who founded the Medical Cadet Corps and commanded it for a quarter of a century, agreed that the camp should have no other name but Camp Desmond T. Doss. Its first session at the permanent home at Grand Ledge, Michigan, was held in June 1951. Desmond was convalescing at Swannanoa, but he still managed to get a furlough for the entire two weeks' duration of the camp. Trim and military in summer uniform, he was active in every phase of the camp's activities, but his greatest contribution was in just being there. He walked around and visited with the cadets. He was their idol; they loved to talk with him.

For the demonstrations which concluded the camp, Desmond not only stood on the reviewing stand, he helped build it.

Desmond with the Freedom Foundation group reporting to
President Nixon after they returned from Vietnam in 1969.
Kenneth D. Walls (facing this way) was a prominent figure in
getting this good will tour together. (Courtesy Del E. Webb
Memorial Library, Loma Linda University, California.)

The Sabbath services were conducted by Elder Haynes. Midway through his sermon the old gentleman suffered a fainting spell. Desmond took over immediately. Within less than a minute a litter was on hand. With Desmond at one post, the unconscious man was carried off to a shady spot.

"Loosen his collar," Desmond directed, "raise his feet." Soon Elder Haynes was back on his feet again as good as new, and Desmond Doss, having plied both his civilian trade of carpenter and his Army specialty as first-aid man, in addition to having inspired his company of cadets for two weeks, went on back to Swannanoa Hospital to continue his convalescence from the removal of a lung and five ribs.

At Fort Sam Houston, Texas, where most Adventists are sent for training in the Medical Department, the rookies are high in their praise of the Medical Cadet Corps training in general, and of the intensive two-week course put on at Camp Desmond T. Doss in particular. In these courses the cadet is taught not only how to serve as a conscientious cooperator but the full philosophical meaning of why.

"The things I learned in the MCC about why we're noncombatants and why we keep the Sabbath have been a real help to me in my Army service," said one young man on completing his basic training.

"It gave me a head start," said another. "By the time I got to Fort Sam Houston, I was already in the know on some military matters."

And another: "Sure, Camp Doss was sort of rough, but it wasn't anything compared with the real thing a little later when Uncle Sam called. I appreciated the training and preparation I got in the MCC."

Since its inception in January of 1934, the MCC has trained approximately 30,000 men in North America and another 12,000 in various overseas divisions. More than 1,000 take MCC training in the United States each year. Similar programs were being conducted in 1967 in South Korea, the Philippines, South Vietnam, Malaysia, Brazil, and Trinidad.

Through the spring of 1967, four young Adventists, including Curtis Reed, had won the Bronze Star for valor as medical aid men. Specialist 4th Class Melvin E. Kohltfarber from Battle Ground, Washington, was on a patrol with his unit near Bao Cap when a large force of Viet Cong attacked with automatic and small arms weapons and mortars. Many Americans were wounded. Kohltfarber, moving from man to man, received a serious wound in his leg from an exploding mortar shell. Bleeding badly and in great pain, he treated his wounds as quickly as he could, then continued to take care of his wounded comrades. He refused to be evacuated until other medics came up to carry on his work.

Another hero, Pfc Fred Villanueva, serving in Vietnam with the 4th Cavalry Regiment, was on patrol with a group of armored vehicles when they ran into a withering hail of grenade and automatic weapons fire. There were several casualties. Villanueva, deliberately leaving the comparative safety of his armored vehicle, went from one to another, braving the swarm of bullets that followed him, to attend to the wounded men. He was climbing aboard one tank to reach the wounded men inside when one of the enemy threw a hand grenade at him. Several fragments struck him and knocked him off the tank. He got up, climbed back on, and took care of the wounded man. He continued on, treating every other wounded man in the unit, before he stopped to care for his own wounds.

The fourth Seventh-day Adventist hero in Vietnam shared some of that ostracism which Desmond Doss had first suffered. When George M. "Mike" Vartenuk of Suffield, Ohio, joined the 5th Mechanized Unit of the 25th Infantry Division, he found that he was the first conscientious objector to serve with the unit.

"Where's your rifle?" the platoon sergeant demanded. "Don't you know there's a war on?"

Mike didn't argue. He knew that before long he would be given an opportunity to prove that even the unarmed could serve. That opportunity arrived just three days later. He treated a wounded soldier and brought him back through a hail of enemy bullets. A few days after that the sergeant himself stopped a bullet in the leg. Mike went out to him, put a dressing on the wound, and carried the sergeant to safety.

Then the 25th Division was assigned the job of cleaning out the infamous Iron Triangle, a jungle area north of Saigon. Mike's company, composed of armored personnel carriers, was hit by a Viet Cong ambush. The VC were throwing everything they had. An enemy shell blew the track off the lead vehicle and the entire column came to a halt.

Another shell landed in the vehicle behind Mike Vartenuk. A case of mortar fuses started burning. Seven men were trapped inside the vehicle, along with some sixty mortar shells. Mike ran to the blazing vehicle. He pulled out two men who were blocking the exit. He went into the hot, smoky interior again and again, until every man was safe.

Just as Desmond Doss maintained that he did not save as many men as the officers said, so Mike insists that, contrary to reports, he did not go into the blazing vehicle seven separate times. "I think some of the men got out by themselves," he said.

In addition to pulling whatever number out of the vehicle, he also pulled them away from it before it exploded. And though bullets were buzzing through the air, Mike gave blood plasma to four of the men, standing up, holding the bottle high so that the plasma would run down into their veins.

After that there was no more ostracism for Mike Vartenuk. Men sought him out, asked him to tell them about his religion. And when the tough sergeant who had criticized the unarmed medic that first day left Vietnam, he made a special effort to say good-bye to Mike Vartenuk.

"I want you to come visit me when you get home," the sergeant said, "You're welcome there anytime."

There will probably always be men like Doss and Vartenuk, misunderstood Christians who must prove themselves and their motives to their fellow soldiers. But because of their very actions, their complete acceptance has become and will continue to be, in Army language, more and more SOP—standing operating procedure (or standard operating procedure).

The influence and inspiration of Desmond Doss extend into groups other than the military, and even beyond the shores of his country. His exploits have been told the world over. No one can guess how many persons have been, and will be in years to come, introduced to Adventism and encouraged to join the movement, directly or indirectly, through his faith and heroism.

When Desmond first saw Okinawa, for example, there was not one Seventh-day Adventist on that faraway little island. After the war a mission was established, and soon a school and medical center were thriving there. Okinawan church members erected two markers, one with English wording, one with Japanese, commemorating Desmond's exploits.

While gathering information for this book, Booton Herndon helps Doss nail roofing material on Doss's Lookout Mountain church. Both men are Virginians; both are veterans. Herndon served with the Army in Europe.

The United States government erected two monuments at the escarpment site after the war. One plaque is in English, the other in Japanese. The original brass plaques were later stolen, marble ones now replacing them.

Pfc. Desmond T. Doss

This Seventh-day Adventist Medical aid man of the 77th Infantry Division received the Congressional Medal of Honor for Valor during the battle for the Maeda Escarpment. Pfc Doss remained on top of the escarpment after his unit was driven off, searched for the wounded men, carried 75 of them to the edge of the cliff and lowered them over the side in a rope litter.

This marble plaque on the monument at the escarpment pays tribute to the heroism of Desmond Doss.

The little Okinawan church has even had its own small miracle, the miracle of the papaya trees. An older woman who first bitterly opposed the church became converted and gave two of her ten papaya trees to the church. The other eight trees bore only a few small fruit, but the two trees which belonged to the Lord delivered 140 papayas in all, each weighing four to five pounds!

On Okinawa, as on Guam and Leyte, Desmond felt that caring for his buddies he was under the shadow of the Almighty. But even if he was killed, he believed, his death would be in a good cause if it occurred while he was caring for his fellow man as Jesus Christ had done.

Desmond Doss did not die, but lived to receive one of the highest of temporal honors. Though they have suffered adversities, he and Dorothy have lived to see positive and increasing results of his heroism and sacrifice. He has continued to serve God and man. In conflict he found encouragement in the ninety-first and ninety-third psalms. In his peaceful life on Lookout Mountain his faith and his actions continue to be steadfast. They repeat what the psalmist sang:

*Thy testimonies are very sure: holiness becometh Thine house,*
*O LORD, forever.*

# EPILOGUE

## by Les Speer

I had recently returned from teaching in a college in Africa where we had to face terrorism on a daily basis.

Sitting on Desmond's front porch I told of torture, rape, and killing in the community where we lived. Radio Maputo had announced that our Solusi College faculty would be killed and the students "liberated." Our faculty was mostly white, and all students were African of many different nationalities. We understood that this broadcast meant that our young men would be forced to be "freedom fighters" (terrorists) or be killed, and the young ladies would be expected to satisfy the young men's sexual desires. I told Desmond of my struggle with the decision to purchase a local version of the Israeli Uzi to defend my family and my students. Desmond listened quietly for quite a while then remarked, "In a different kind of war, I might have made a different decision." I found that response very insightful and rather broadminded.

After Desmond's enlistment, in the early years of the war, he was branded a "Pacifist." Desmond resented the label, repeatedly explaining that he was a "Conscientious Cooperator." The brand never gained traction. He wanted to serve his country, he wanted to care for the men who were fighting for American principles and freedoms. His fellow soldiers came to respect, admire and champion Desmond as an exemplary American patriot. Desmond understood his status of "Hero" in the eyes of others, but he was uncomfortable with the accolade and always identified the real heroes as the men he served with, especially those who lost their lives. Up to his death, this humble, selfless man of great faith credited God with his courage, bravery, valor under fire, and his survival.

When Desmond returned from the war, and after his five and one half years of recovery in hospitals and special therapy, he received mixed response from the typical American. Some Americans did not appreciate

Desmond and Dorothy Doss assist in the dedication of the Desmond T. Doss Medal of Honor Highway, in 1990, Walker County, Georgia. (Courtesy Del E. Webb Memorial Library, Loma Linda University, California.)

Desmond's non-combat status during the war. But most people were happy to honor a war hero. Through the years, Desmond's picture was on the front pages of many city newspapers from coast to coast—in Memorial Day parades, or speaking to school assemblies, public and parochial, faith communities of varied denominations, and youth fraternal organizations such as Boy Scouts. When he went to the annual Medal of Honor Society conventions, it was very common for the other recipients of the Congressional Medal of Honor to get in line to talk to their hero, Desmond Doss. When group pictures were taken, Desmond's fellow Medal of Honor recipients often asked Desmond to stand in the front row. It was common for a simple trip to the grocery store to turn into a long visit with a passerby who noticed Desmond's Medal of Honor license plate. He never seemed distressed when a crowd sometimes wanted to spend 20 or 30 minutes visiting with him, a quiet humble man. One soldier told me that Desmond was one of the greatest heroes of our nation, yet Desmond treated this private as if he was the hero.

Desmond Doss, Sr., loved America more than anyone I have ever met. To go into his living room was to be greeted by perhaps 25 or 30 American

Doss and first wife Dorothy (Shutte) in a family portrait. Desmond was rarely without his Medal of Honor. Suffering from severe hearing loss as a result of the side effects of medicine used to treat the tuberculosis he contracted during the war, Doss eventually had cochlear implant surgery. (Courtesy Del E. Webb Memorial Library, Loma Linda University, California.)

flags. One flag had flown over the nation's Capitol building and one over the Georgia Capitol building. Instead of a group of flowers, there was a bouquet of flags in a large cluster.

---

In 1976 Desmond became totally deaf, presumably from massive doses of streptomycin used to treat the tuberculosis contracted during the war. Desmond's wife, Dorothy, a registered nurse, became his ears. During conversations with friends or in church, she wrote out thousands of pages of conversation so Desmond could know what was being said. A new medical treatment, cochlear implant, became available in 1988. A number of small miracles combined to allow Desmond to be able to get this new surgery at Loma Linda University Hospital in California free of charge. Transportation, travel expenses, housing, and an apartment to live in were provided by the veteran's administration, Chattanooga military groups, and Dorothy's family members. The recovery took months, but Desmond could hear again after 12 years! Now Desmond's struggle was to interpret the "Donald Duck" sounds from his implant into meaningful conversation. Most people talked too fast and high pitched for Desmond to understand. If a person would lower his or her voice in pitch, slow the speed and face Desmond so he could lip read, it was possible to carry on a meaningful conversation.

In 1991, Desmond's wife, Dorothy, was diagnosed with cancer. She was a BS RN and knew the struggle ahead. Within a year, both Desmond's and Dorothy's mothers had died from cancer. Dorothy believed that if she put off surgery as long as possible, it would give her the best quality of life. She had hospital treatment, but was not operated on. I think it was November 17 when Dorothy decided it was time to go to the hospital—with the likelihood that she would have surgery. Dorothy was a very strong person and only severe pain would move her to make this decision. It was a rainy morning as I remember. Desmond drove toward town. He was not going fast. At one point he applied the brakes on a curve, the car's tires may have hydroplaned and perhaps got the wheel off the pavement. He lost control and the car went over the embankment and a telephone pole hit Dorothy's side of the car, and she died. Having seen death so often in World War II, he checked her but saw there was no hope. 911 was called and the jaws of life tore the car apart to get her out. This was an extremely deep loss for Desmond. A few days later, I took him to the funeral home and

Desmond at the grave of Dorothy P. (Schutte) Doss, Chattanooga National Cemetery, Tennessee. (Courtesy Del E. Webb Memorial Library, Loma Linda University, California.)

Chattanooga National Cemetery in my car because he did not have a car and did not want to drive.

After making his selection of a grave site for his bride, he sat in the back of my small car and wept for a long time. I waited until he was ready to go. At last he paused and said, "I was just counting my blessings. At least she is not suffering and she did not have to have surgery."

Desmond found it almost torture to stay at home without Dorothy. He called me and asked if he might stay with us for a while. We gladly welcomed him and after a few days tried to teach him how to make some of his favorite meals. He had never prepared his own meals, other than a snack, and it was hard to get him to think about fixing meals for himself.

Desmond and Francis (Duman) Doss happily pose for the photographer in their home, Rising Fawn, Georgia. (Courtesy Del E. Webb Memorial Library, Loma Linda University, California.)

To Desmond and Frances Doss
With appreciation and best wishes,

Medal of Honor recipients are traditionally invited to presidential inaugurations. Desmond is known to have attended at least six. Desmond and his second wife, Frances, pose with President George W. Bush.

Even when Desmond was in a big crowd, he was still very lonely. After a few months he began to consider remarriage—if he could find the right person. About two years after Dorothy's passing, he fell in love with Frances Duman. They were married July 1, 1993. Now his new bride became his ears and wrote out conversations and sermons. This was not a burden for Frances; she enjoyed doing it for him. It was a great joy to watch them in love. At meal time they would always hold hands while giving thanks for the food, then kiss, then eat.

In 1999 Desmond was diagnosed with bladder cancer. While in radiation treatment, he was weak and unable to keep food down. A lifelong passion for Desmond was supporting his church's version of boy and girl scouts called Pathfinders. During his treatments he was invited to the National Pathfinder Camporee at Oshkosh, Wisconsin. It often had 22,000 to 30,000 young people from 53 countries in attendance. He always enjoyed being with the young people, and they seemed to just adore him. At times, 200 to 400 youth would stand in line to talk with Desmond or

Desmond and Frances Doss (left) with elementary and middle school aged children and their teachers in front of the Desmond T. Doss Seventh-day Adventist School, Lynchburg, Virginia. (Courtesy Del E. Webb Memorial Library, Loma Linda University, California.)

Desmond and second wife Frances, as parade Grand Marshals, during one of hundreds of parades in which Doss participated across America. (Courtesy Del E. Webb Memorial Library, Loma Linda University, California.)

Desmond and his aging father Thomas Doss share a moment together. A difficult and turbulent childhood relationship was forgotten and a complete reconciliation marked their postwar years. (Courtesy Del E. Webb Memorial Library, Loma Linda University, California.)

get his autograph. This trip was almost canceled due to Desmond's health problems. But the Lord gave Desmond health for the trip. He had none of the normal symptoms of his radiation treatments. This year when Desmond stepped onto the stage, 22,000 Pathfinders gave him a long standing ovation. Then he received the highest award possible in Pathfinding— they made him an Honorary Master Guide. A Master Guide is required to pass a number of classes and read lots of books, etc. Because Desmond was a slow reader, he had never completed the course work required. He was thrilled with this honor.

Every time I witnessed Desmond's telling of his story of God's protection in battle, the crowd of perhaps 250 Pathfinders and parents were almost spellbound. Normally kids that age would be wiggly and somewhat noisy, but not when Desmond was speaking. The crowd of kids was as quiet as mice under hypnosis.

A bronze depiction of Doss lowering a wounded man over the escarpment. The rope was wrapped around a tree stump to add mechanical advantage to slow his patient's descent. (Courtesy Del E. Webb Memorial Library, Loma Linda University, California.)

Through the years many companies and individuals had tried to buy the rights to Desmond's story for a Hollywood movie. According to Desmond, they wanted to get the story and then make it into an exciting fiction thriller, like most films, to make lots of money. This idea was very painful to Desmond. He said, "My story is not about me so much as it is about the God that I serve. When I was on the escarpment, after the first two or three men that I dragged on the ground to the edge, after the first few trips on the ground, I stood up while carrying men, with no attempt to avoid bullets. I figured if God had protected me on the first few, He might protect me for the rest. I just kept praying Lord, help me get one more, and after that one, help me get one more, until they were all down. In my mind I felt I would be killed up on top, but I was at peace with that if that was God's will for me." So he felt that somehow he needed to protect his

Desmond demonstrates the double bowline knot he used to safely lower wounded soldiers down the Maeda Escarpment's vertical face. The knot can be tied quickly, remains tight without slipping under load, and can be released quickly and easily.

story from fiction and from companies who just wanted to make money from it. In fact, the offers to buy his story would have been enough to make Desmond comfortable for the rest of his life, but in the end he turned each offer down because the "would-be producers" were not willing to be totally honest with him, or produce an accurate retelling of what God had done in his life. Perhaps some felt they could exploit this simple country boy, but he had a will of iron and would not compromise his convictions.

So, in 2000, all rights to his story including movie rights and book rights were given to the Georgia-Cumberland Association of Seventh-day Adventists. The terms of his gift were that the Association would preserve, protect and manage Desmond's story, intellectual property, collections and memorabilia, and would use any proceeds to teach character development to young people and to honor God. In time a Desmond T. Doss Council was established, and their first big project was to make a documentary of Desmond's story while he yet lived. Desmond, with Frances's assistance, attended as many of the production meetings as his health allowed, offering suggestions and approving content. The documentary was a huge success. Terry Benedict was the director and the documentary received many awards at film festivals. The documentary proved popular with veterans. It has been shown on national television over a dozen times and on Armed Forces Network and the Pentagon Channel several times. The distribution has been international.

After the documentary, Desmond was willing, but cautious, about a movie of his experiences. As a final decision on a movie he stipulated that the Doss Council could authorize a movie if it glorified God and would teach young people to trust in the Lord. In time, and initially, the story rights for a movie were assigned to Pandemonium Films and Waldon Media. After nearly eleven years of patient waiting and on-again, off-again activity, a production entity was created, funded and green-lighted. Actual filming began in Australia in the fall of 2015, with Bill Mechanic producing, Mel Gibson directing and Andrew Garfield playing the role of Desmond Doss.

---

Part of the treatment to conquer Desmond's tuberculosis was to remove his left lung. This left him short of breath much of the time. He had a slight build and only weighed perhaps 145 or 150 pounds most of his life. In his later years, he would ride the riding lawn mower from the house to his shed 300 feet away. His yard was large, and because of his shortness of breath and his failing eyesight, it became too much for him to keep up. So the decision was made to move next to Frances's son, Mike Duman, in Piedmont, Alabama. There were boxes of pictures, newspaper articles and other mementos, all of which needed to be preserved somehow. In the preparation for moving, a small room was kept for memorabilia of all kinds. These collections entrusted to the Desmond Doss Council were collated and are housed in the archival Heritage Room of the Del E. Webb Memorial Library, Loma Linda University, California. The collection contains pictures of Desmond Doss, Sr., with six United States presidents and a host of important and precious people from around the world.

Desmond's health gradually deteriorated until his death on March 23, 2006. He was 87 years old. His grave is close to the Medal of Honor tree near the top of the hill in the Chattanooga National Cemetery, Tennessee.

> One of Desmond Doss's favorite Scripture quotes: "Trust in the Lord with all thine heart; and lean not on thine own understanding. In all thy ways acknowledge Him, and He shall direct thy paths." Proverbs 3:5, 6

Les Speer is a Georgia-Cumberland Association Trust Officer and was Desmond Doss's pastor for several years.

# INDEX

# INDEX